Policies and Practices
in Evening Colleges 1969

By the
Research Committee of the
Association of University Evening Colleges

William A. Hoppe, Editor

The Scarecrow Press, Inc.

Metuchen, N.J.

SBN 8108-0278-3

Table of Contents

3

4

B. Can you, as director of the evening division, reject a faculty member who has been assigned to teach evening classes?
C. Do you employ any full-time faculty members who teach exclusively in the evening?
D. Can you, as evening director engage an instructor without the consent of the department head if this person refuses to staff these classes?
E. Do you hold regular faculty meetings with your evening faculty?
F. What are your policies regarding regular faculty members teaching credit or non-credit courses or participating in institutes, seminars and conferences as an overload?

A. Offering credit and/or non-credit courses in "store front" locations off-campus for economically deprived populations?
B. To what extent do students at your institution participate in any discussion regarding the academic program? How do they participate?

5

Part Six: General Comments (cont.)

7

Individual Colleges and Schools
Responding to Survey (cont.)

* Name will change to Old Dominion University,
  September 1, 1969.

Preface

This survey of "Policies and Practices in Various Evening Colleges and Divisions of Colleges and Universities in the United States" was made by the Research Committee of the Association of University Evening Colleges in the interest of evening divisions and colleges throughout the country. Members of the AUEC Research Committee included: Dr. Glenn L. Bushey, Dean of Chattanooga College, University of Chattanooga; Mr. D. David Hughes, Director of Evening Classes, University of Georgia; Mr. Paul V. Trovillo, Coordinator of Continuing Education, St. Petersburg Junior College; Dr. Eugene Upshaw, Director of the Nashville Center, University of Tennessee; Dr. William A. Hoppe, Associate Dean of Arts & Sciences, University of South Alabama, Chairman.

Questionnaires were sent to colleges and universities throughout the United States and Canada--including the entire membership of the Association of University Evening Colleges. A total of 107 institutions responded including the following:

State Universities	26	Private Colleges	64
State Colleges	8	Church-related	22
Junior Colleges	9	Private Colleges	20
		Private Univ's	22

Total 107

As Chairman of the AUEC Research Committee, I wish to thank each evening college dean or director that responded to the questionnaire--without their interest and cooperation this study would not have been possible. We trust that you will find the results interesting and that each of you will be able to use this survey to advantage.

I wish to thank the members of the AUEC Research Committee for their advice and assistance in completing this study. Finally, I wish to express my appreciation to Dr. Raymond P. Witte, Director of the Evening Division of Loyola University (New Orleans), and President-elect of AUEC for his advice and encouragement. He gave his wholehearted support to this study, and it was his decision to distribute the complete results of the study to the entire membership of AUEC.

11

Conclusions

This study included seven general areas: I. Admission Policies; II. Terminology; III. Fees; IV. Faculty and Faculty Recruitment; V. Scheduling; Research; VI. General Policies; and VII. Student Recruitment (Or Publicity). A few important conclusions might be reached by examining the summary material as follows:

I. Admission Policies

The results show that most institutions have flexible admission policies for adults to allow them to take credit courses as part-time degree students or "special" or non-degree students.

a. 53 institutions (49%) have no deadline for applications or allow one week for applications to be completed.

b. 83 institutions (77%) allow adults to register for credit courses without submitting a transcript including 13% provisional registration. In some instances, they are tentatively classified as "special" or "non-degree" students who must be matriculated as degree students after completing a certain number of hours with satisfactory grades.

c. Approximately 86% of the institutions will allow an adult to register as a "special" or non-degree student--and students may take from 8 hours to an indefinite number of hours before being required to matriculate as degree students.

d. 48% of the institutions allow students to register for credit courses by mail.

e. 75% of the institutions allow special students to take credit courses without taking a standard examination such as ACT or CEEB as degree and/or "special" students.

f. 24 institutions offer special degree programs for adults--28 additional institutions are considering offering special degree programs.

II. Terminology

28 titles are used to designate the division, school or

12

college used to serve the academic needs of adults.

III. Fees

51 institutions charge lower fees for evening students; 53 institutions charge the same fees.

IV. Faculty and Faculty Recruitment

1. Most institutions have no fixed policies regarding the percentage of full-time faculty teaching evening classes. However, only 41 institutions (38%), have less than 50% full-time faculty teaching in the evening.

2. In 37 institutions (34%), the Director or Dean has the responsibility for hiring full-time faculty; in 41 institutions (38%), the department chairman has this responsibility.

V. a. Scheduling

1. The director or dean of the evening division, school or college is responsible for the evening class schedule in 85 institutions. In 43 institutions (40%) department heads submit evening class schedules for the Director's or Dean's approval. Consideration is given to student needs, faculty availability, space limitations, past class enrollments, and budget limitations.

V. b. Research

24 institutions reported research projects in adult education either completed or in progress. The Research Committee has received copies of research results from several institutions. The committee plans to recommend that some of the research results be made available to AUEC members as well as other evening colleges and universities.

VI. General Policies

1. Evening college administrators should be particularly interested in some of the innovative practices listed for 37 institutions including Headstart and Upward Bound programs, a tutorial project operating in 10 ghetto locations, a

13

Model Cities Leadership Program, and other interesting projects.

2. Students are allowed to participate fully in discussions regarding the academic program in only 29 institutions (27%); in 42 institutions (39%), students do not participate in any discussions of the academic program.

3. 58% of the institutions reported that their Evening Division or College was receiving adequate support; 75% of the institutions stated that the administration in their institution recognized the need and importance of the adult education program.

VII. Student Recruitment

Most institutions make full use of the newspaper for publicity purposes. Only 18% of the institutions make use of television for publicity purposes.

Summary of the Survey

I. Admission Policies

I. Do you have a deadline for applications for admission to evening classes ___49___ vs. ___41___
                              Yes   No

II. If so, what is the deadline?

One month __8__ University of Kentucky; St. Joseph's College, University College of the University of Syracuse; Rutgers University, Marquette University, DePaul University; University of Toledo; Manhattan College.

1 to 3 mo. __10__ Sir George Williams University, Polytech. Institute of Brooklyn, University of Windsor, University of Toronto, City College of New York (some exceptions made), Iona College, University College of the University of Southern California, University of Bridgeport, Ohio State University, Drexel Institute of Technology.

14

3 to 8 mos.	7	The American University, Brooklyn College of City University of New York, Queensborough Community College, Nassau County Community College, Newark State College, Springfield College, Newark College of Engineering.
1 week	11	LaSalle College, Hofstra University, The Citadel, Indiana Central College, Northwestern University, Philadelphia College of Textiles and Science, Roosevelt University, American International College, University of Maryland, Peirce Junior College, St. Bonaventure University (3 days prior to classes).
2 weeks	6	Washington University (St. Louis), East Tennessee State University, University of Akron, Bryant College, University of Chattanooga, Univ. of Georgia.
3 weeks	4	University of Southern Mississippi, School of Continuing Education and Extension Services of New York University, Washburn University of Topeka, New Haven University.
No deadline (Some through late registration period)	41	University of Cincinnati, Old Dominion College, Community College of Baltimore, Brigham Young University, Loyola Evening College (Baltimore), Louisiana State University (Baton Rouge), Texas Christian University, Loyola University (New Orleans), McNeese State College, Memphis State College, Millikin University, University of Minnesota, C. W. Post College, Boston College, Miami-Dade Junior College, Metropolitan College of St. Louis University, University of Tampa, Virginia Commonwealth University, Johns Hopkins University, Purdue University-Calumet Campus, Rochester Institute of Technology, Northern Virginia University, Trenton State College, Cleveland College of Case Western Reserve University, Drury College, Pace College, University of North Carolina, Babson Institute of Education, Orange County Community College, University of Tennessee (Knoxville), Louisiana State University (New Orleans),

15

No deadline <u>41</u>   St. Francis College, University of South-
(cont.)   ern California-University College, Univer-
             sity of Louisville, Springfield College
             (None for special students) Southern Con-
             necticut State College, Dutchess Commu-
             nity College, Bloomfield College.
May enter after
classes begin <u>5</u>   University of Illinois, Northeastern Uni-
             versity, Roanoke College, Univ. of Tulsa,
             Thomas More College.

III. May a student register for credit courses before transcripts are submitted?

<u> 69 </u>   <u> 22 </u>   <u> 14 </u>
Yes   No   Provisionally

IV. May a student take a certain amount of work for credit
as a non-matriculating or "special" student?

<u> 93 </u>   <u> 5 </u>   <u> 2 </u>
Yes   No   Provisionally

If so, how many hours may be taken?

10-20   <u>22 </u>
Thomas More College, Newark State College, Virginia Commonwealth University, Washburn University
of Topeka, Johns Hopkins University (Additional
courses may be taken but not towards a degree),
College of William and Mary, University of Louisville, University of Akron, Purdue University-Calu-
met Campus, Rochester Institute of Technology, University of Windsor, American International College,
University of Tampa, The New School, Memphis
State University, Miami-Dade Junior College, Nassau
Community College, Peirce Junior College, University of Denver, St. Bonaventure University (for certification), Newark College of Engineering.

21-30   <u>11 </u>   Rutgers University, Indiana Central College,
Roanoke College, American University, New Haven
College, Roosevelt University, Pace College, Suffolk
University, Springfield College (Mass.), Drake Uni-
versity, Southern Connecticut State College.

16

31-60 __8__ Washington University, DePaul University, Rockford College, Manhattan College, Northern Virginia Community College, Western New England College, Cleveland College, Philadelphia College of Textiles and Science.

61-95 __4__ Old Dominion College, Loyola Evening College (Baltimore), University of Tennessee (Knoxville), Drury College.

Other __1__ University of Southern California (University College) - Three Graduate courses or four undergraduate courses.

No
Limit __31__ University of Kentucky, University of Cincinnati, University of Chattanooga, University of Illinois, Queensborough Community College, Community College of Baltimore, Brooklyn College of City University of New York, Brigham Young University, Louisiana State University (Baton Rouge), Texas Christian University, Marquette University, University of Minnesota, University of Maryland, Ohio State University, Metropolitan College (St. Louis), East Tennessee State University, School of General Studies of Columbia University (With B. A. or B. S. degrees), Loyola University (Chicago), Wayne State University, Dutchess Community College, Sir George Williams University, Trenton State College, University of British Columbia, Boston University (Metropolitan College), Polytech Institute of Brooklyn, Orange County Community College, Carnegie Mellon University, Northeastern University, Bronx Community College, City College of New York, Northwestern University, Boston College, University of Georgia, (when taken for personal or professional improvement only).

V. What are the admission requirements for:

A. Non-matriculating or "special" students?

   1. H. S. graduation, GED, and/or entrance examination (one school - may enter with advanced standing) __22__
   2. H. S. graduation, GED (some schools require

A. Non-matriculating or "special" students? (cont.)
   a certain %age score), and, if applicable, a
   college transcript.   24
   3. Sufficient background to pass the course(s)   22
   4. 18 yrs or H. S. graduation   2
   5. 19 yrs, H. S. graduation   9
   6. 21 yrs, H. S. graduation   5
   7. High school graduate, GED or mature person
      with special needs or interests   3
   8. Satisfactory H. S. record (some schools require
      specific GPA, and evidence of preparation   5
   9. Statement from previous institution that student
      is in good standing   6
  10. Upper 3/4 of H. S. graduating class, acceptable
      GED, or good standing from another college   2
  11. H. S. certificate (specific units specified)   1
  12. Students with B. A. or B. S. degree   3
  13. Other special requirements   5

B. Degree Students

   1. High school graduate or GED   30
      American International College (Bus. major),
      Northeastern University, Ohio State University, Or-
      ange County Community College (plus SUNY exam),
      Peirce Junior College, Johns Hopkins University
      (meet course prerequisites), Old Dominion College,
      Hofstra University (advisement test), University of
      Toledo (or college transcripts), Trenton State Col-
      lege, Bryant College, University of Cincinnati, The
      Citadel (or college transcripts), Dutchess Community
      College, Roanoke College (or college transcripts),
      Rochester Institute of Technology, L. S. U. - Baton
      Rouge (in good standing), Loyola Evening College
      (Baltimore), Loyola University (New Orleans), Loy-
      ola University (Chicago) - or college transcripts,
      McNeese State College, Miami-Dade Junior College,
      New Haven College, Northwestern University, Univer-
      sity of Richmond (or college transcripts), St. Joseph's
      College (grades of 80), University of Southern Mis-
      sissippi, Washington University (St. Louis), Spring-
      field College (Massachusetts), University of Georgia
      (and acceptable SAT Scores).

   2. High School graduate (satisfactory grades or
      certain GPA), ACT, CEEB, or SAT (Min.
      scores Usually)   17

18

Boston University (Metropolitan College), Iona College, Nassau Community College, Roosevelt University, Manhattan College, Suffolk University (CEEB-SAT waived for mature students), Tampa University, University of Tulsa, Washburn University of Topeka, University of Chattanooga, American University, Bloomfield College, Indiana Central College, Columbia University (General Studies), Memphis State University, Southern Connecticut State College, University College of Syracuse University.

3. High school graduate, 15-16 units (some schools specify), and satisfactory performance on ACT, CEEB, SAT.   6
Bronx Community College, University of Denver, Pace College, Philadelphia College of Textiles and Science, Brigham Young University, Newark‾ College.

4. Class rank required, ACT, CEEB or SAT (Min. scores), High school graduate   9
Carnegie-Mellon University, Newark State College, University of North Carolina, Northern Illinois University, Brooklyn College of City University of N. Y., DePaul University, University of Louisville (No CEEB or SAT) - rank only, Millikin University, Rutgers University (University College).

5. High school graduate with specific course requirements and/or units or GPA.   9
American International College (Arts & Sciences), Brooklyn Polytech Institute, St. Francis College, Western New England College, University of Bridgeport, Boston College, Centenary College, C. W. Post College, Drexel Institute of Technology.

6. High School graduate or college transcripts, CEEB, ACT, SAT (Minimum scores)   3
University of Akron, Cleveland College of Western Reserve University, Drury College.

7. No admission requirements   4
Harvard University (Extension), University of Minnesota, Northern Virginia Community College, Texas Christian University.

B. Degree Students (cont.)

    8. Same as for day students   <u>5</u>

    9. Upper 1/2 of class or upper 1/2 of national
average on SAT   <u>1</u>
Purdue University - Calumet Campus

  10. Grade 13 with 60% or 7 papers   <u>1</u>
University of Windsor

  11. Other   <u>5</u>
New York University (School of Continuing Education & Extension Services)
Associate in Arts & Associate in Science (Business): high school certificate, or GED, performance on adult admission text equivalent to level required for admission to other undergraduate degree programs, intensive interview (some programs require SAT scores).
Associate in Applied Science in Early Childhood Education and Social Work-Day program for adults; high school certificate or GED (or provisional admission subject to earning GED within one year), satisfactory performance on adult admissions test, intensive interview.

VI. Some junior and senior colleges and universities are now registering students for credit courses by mail. Do you use mail registration at your institution? <u>52</u> If so, what procedure is used? (Limited examples <u>Yes</u> listed below)

    1. Materials are mailed at same time catalog is sent. Instructions are included. Mail registrations are accepted up to a date approximately one week prior to the opening of the semester. (Washington University, St. Louis)

    2. All new and continuing students may register by mail. A period during the semester is designated as pre-programming for mail registration. During this period, all students wishing to take advantage of mail registration are programmed by their appropriate advisor and are billed later. (C. W. Post College)

20

3. Registrar mails registration material to all students in attendance but only those who have formal plan of studies made by a faculty advisor and filed in the University College Office may return the material by mail. Registration is checked in the office against this plan of studies (student has one copy of it for reference in filling out registration forms). These mail registrants may register in advance of other continuing students. (Hofstra University)

4. Course selection forms and schedules of classes are mailed to all students. These are filled out and mailed to the college. The Dean and Assistant Dean approve (or disapprove) every form. All cards are mailed to the student. The student fills them out and mails them back to the college along with the check for tuition. (Loyola Evening College, Baltimore)

5. Students request mail registration kit--completes and returns it and staff processes the registration in advance of regular registration date. (Texas Christian University)

6. New students see a counselor to assist them in completing a scheduling card (if eligible) and are given a mail packet for completion and return. Former students may telephone and designate course selection. Schedule card and mail packet are mailed for completion and returned. (Cleveland College of Case Western Reserve University)

7. Printed form in newspaper; in evening brochure; and separate form. Mail registrations are accepted three to four weeks prior to "in person" registration. (University College of the University of Richmond)

8. Currently, all former students registered during the previous quarter receive a packet of IBM forms and course information allowing them to register completely by mail. (Northeastern University)

9. Mail registration cards are sent to previous registrants and others upon request, full fee must accompany returned cards. Cards are returned to the University Registrar's Office. (University of British Columbia)

VI. Mail registration examples (cont.)

    10. Students mail course selections to computer section. On registration day students pay their bills and are given schedule. First-time students cannot use this method. (St. Bonaventure University)

VII. What are the retention policies for your evening students?

    A. Regular Students

1. Grade point average of "C"	34
2. Satisfactory grades or making progress towards a degree	7
3. No retention policy	8
4. Same as for day students	4
5. Varies according to school	3
6. Certain GPA according to number of hours student has taken or year enrolled (Limited examples listed below)	32

1. 1.6 in freshman year; 1.8 in sophomore year; 2.0 in junior and senior years. (Bloomfield College), (East Tennessee State College, Knoxville).

2. 16 hours--1.00 average; 17-48 hours--1.35 average; 2.00 after 90 hours, (Trenton State College).

3. Probation at 6-12 QP deficiency; dismissed at 13 QP deficiency, (University of Louisville).

4. Dependent on GPA after 12 credit hours; dismissed or suspended if less than 1.75 out of 4.00 after two semesters (Orange County Community College).

5. Three "F's" in semester requires a withdrawal. Student with a "C" average on probation; average of "C" is required for graduation (Boston College).

6. 15 deficiency points and student is suspended (University of Bridgeport).

7. A student who has attempted 72 hours and has not achieved a GPA of 1.5 is excluded (Miami-Dade Jr. College).

22

8. Maintain graduation requirement of 3. 20 average. Probationary limitations imposed on delinquents by faculty committee (Rutgers University).

9. First four semesters in any degree program 1. 8 on 4. 00. Fifth semester and to completion 2. 00. (Rochester Institute of Technology).

10.

12-20	hrs below	. 35	dismissed below	1. 35	academic pro-
21-35	" "	1. 35	"	" 1. 65	" bation
36-50	" "	1. 65	"	" 1. 80	"
51-65	" "	1. 80	"	" 1. 90	"
66-80	" "	1. 90	"	" 2. 00	"
81 or above		1. 95	"	" 2. 00	"

(University of Maryland).

11. Three "F's" in a semester requires a withdrawal. Student with a "C" average on probation; "C" average required for graduation. (Boston College)

   B. Non-degree or "special students" (If different requirements from regular students)
      1. Same policy as for day students -   63
         a. "C" average- 25
         b. "C" average after 24-30 hrs. or 4-6 sems. -10
         c. Graduated grade point average- 23
         d. Passing grades or grades reviewed by committee- 5
      2. No policy or passing grades- 24
      3. "B" average- 1
      4. Other- 8
      5. No "special" students- 4

VIII. Do you require the ACT or CEEB Examination for adults in the Evening Division?

5	7	15	80	2
ACT	CEEB	Yes	No	Occasionally

Are other tests required?	40	63	2
(In place of or in addition to standardized tests)	Yes	No	Occasionally

List of other tests used:

1. SCAT (or ACT, CEEB) - (University of Chattanooga)

23

List of other tests used: (cont.)

2. Reading advisement test - (Hofstra University)
3. Placement tests in English, Math, Language, Speech- (Queensborough Community College)
4. Qualifying examination - (Brooklyn College)
5. For non-high school graduates and scholastically deficient transfers - (Rutgers University)
6. SCAT in place of high school certificate - Loyola University, New Orleans)
7. University's Adult Admission Test - (School of Con. Educ. and Extension Services - New York University)
8. SCAT and Cooperative English Reading Test - (Boston College)
9. University has its own battery of tests - (DePaul University)
10. SAT for matriculation - (Indiana Central College)
11. CEEB Placement tests - (University of Toledo and Purdue University - Calumet Campus)
12. Sometimes C. L. E. P. or reading tests - (Suffolk University)
13. Ohio State Psychological Examination; our own Mechanics of English and English Composition exams; Iowa Math Test and our Math Achievement exam (for those applying for science or mathematics - (LaSalle College)
14. Graduate record for admission to graduate school - (Virginia Commonwealth University)
15. SCAT (and CEEB if less than 3 years since h. s. grad.) - (School of Gen. Studies - Columbia University)
16. At graduate level or for borderline students - (College of William and Mary)
17. Diagnostic tests for some courses - (Dutchess Community College)
18. Only if SAT is not satisfactory - (Pace College)
19. We use our own "mature matriculation battery" - (Sir George Williams University)
20. A mathematics placement test where appropriate - (Rochester Institute of Technology)
21. The Ohio State University Psychological Test. This test is given where there are no other test scores or they are outdated - (Cleveland College of Case Western University)
22. Our own tests - (Philadelphia College of Textiles and Sciences)
23. Sometimes admissions test for graduate study of business - (Babson Institute of Education)
24. Roosevelt University Entrance Exam - (Roosevelt University)

24

25. Graduate record for M. A. students - (American International College)
26. English language ability as indicated - (University of Toronto)
27. SCAT (may change to C. Q. T. exam) - (Newark State College)
28. English and Math - (Northeastern University)
29. New Haven College Placement Tests - (New Haven College)
30. Placement tests in Language, Math, English and Data Processing - (Bronx Community College)
31. CEEB, GRE for undergraduate, or graduate studies - (University of Southern California - University College)
32. In certain areas such as law - (University of Denver)
33. CEEB for degree students, occasionally SCAT - (American University)

Are these tests used as a basis for admission?   47   53
                                                 Yes   No
Or for placement and advisement?   46   40
                                                 Yes   No

IX. Do you offer a special degree program for adults?
                                    24   80
                                    Yes   No
        School Offering a Special Degree Program

Degree	Enrollment	School
1. Bachelor of Science	3,000+	University of Cinn.
2. Special Baccalaureate Degree program for adults	150	Brooklyn College of the City University of New York
3. Bachelor of Sci. in Gen. Studies	1,096	Louisiana State University, Baton Rouge
4. Bachelor of Arts in Lib. Studies	100+	Univ. of Syracuse, University College
5. Bachelor of Arts with divisional concentration in Humanities, Natural Sciences (incl. Math) or Soc. Sci.	1,500	Texas Christian University
6. Bachelor of Arts and Bachelor of Commercial Studies (not the same as day program)	650	Loyola University, New Orleans

School Offering a Special Degree Program (cont.)
7. Associate in Arts in Law Enf. 51   Marquette University
8. Three special degrees for adults:
   Assoc. in Arts (Eve.) 181   New York University, School
   Assoc. in Appl. Sci.   of Continuing Education and
   (Bus. eve.)   132   Extension Services
   Assoc. in Appl. Sci. (Early
   Childhood Ed. and Social
   Wk (day)   60
9. Bachelor of Gen. Studies 550   Roosevelt University
10. Certificate programs in Trans-
    portation, Traffic Management
    and Law Enforcement 550   Bryant College
11. Assoc. degree in Liberal
    Arts; Assoc. degree in
    Business Administration   The Citadel
12. Bachelor of Arts - Gen.
    Studies Curr.   5,000+   University of Maryland
13. A. A. degree   500   Peirce Junior College
14. B. S. in Gen. Studies   29   Suffolk University
15. Certificate in Arts and Sciences
    & Business   7500   Johns Hopkins University
    Master of Liberal Arts Summer- 2500
    Master of Science, major in
    Numerical Science, Physics, Applied Physics
16. B. S. degree   3200   Columbia University-School
                                of Gen. Studies
17. Bachelor of Arts, Bachelor of
    Commerce, Master of Com-
    merce, Master of Humani-
    ties   934   University College of the
                            Univ. of Richmond
18. A. A. degree   150   Rochester Inst. of Tech.
19. Bachelor of Science   180   Drury College
20. Master of Liberal Studies 19   Boston University - Metro-
                                politan College
21. Master of Business Ad-
    ministration   430   Babson Inst. of Education
22. Bachelor of Science in
    General Studies   30   American University
    Master of Science in
    Teaching   82
    B. S. in Law Enforcement 275
    M. S. in Correctional
    Administration   18
23. Assoc. in Applied Science
    (new)   4   Manhattan College
24. A. A. in Extension Studies   Harvard University

Note: Other institutions offering special adult degree programs but not included in this study are: University of Oklahoma, University of South Florida, Goddard College and Queens College.

X. Are you considering offering a special degree program for adults in the near future? <u>28</u> <u>70</u>
                                                            Yes No

1. Univ. of Chattanooga (recommended)
2. Queensborough Community College
3. Texas Christian Univ. (add. prog.)
4. McNeese State College
5. Memphis State University
6. Brigham Young University
7. C. W. Post College
8. University of Southern Mississippi
9. DePaul University
10. Miami-Dade Junior College
11. Univ. of Maryland (considering graduate level M. S. in Soc. Sci., M. A. in Liberal Studies; at undergraduate level, B. A. in Police Science.)
12. Metropolitan College of St. Louis University
13. Suffolk Univ., (Revision of B. S. in Gen. Stu. for flexibility)
14. University of Tampa
15. East Tenn. State Univ. (planning to offer 2 yr. program in chem., accounting, and industrial education.
16. Western New England College (an associate degree in general education after 60-66 hrs. or 3-4 years of evening study.
17. College of William and Mary
18. Rochester Instit. of Tech. (will enlarge majors from General Education to a broad Fine Arts, also)
19. The University of British Columbia
20. The University of North Carolina
21. Thomas More College (Police Science Certificate Program)
22. Newark State College
23. Orange County Community College
24. New Haven College (possibly for adult women)
25. University of Tennessee (Knoxville)
26. St. Francis College
27. University of Southern California (University College)
28. Manhattan College (Hope to offer B. S. in Radiological Health and Sciences as development of the new A. A. S. in the same area)

XI. What are the admission requirements for the special degree program(s)?

Same as for regular students: __6__

Other:

1. Extensive interviews for two days (Syracuse University-University College)

2. Associate in Arts Evening Degree Program for Adults and Associate in Applied Science (Business) Evening Degree Program for Adults: high school graduation or equivalency diploma, performance on adult admissions test equivalent to level required for admission to other undergraduate degree programs (it is hard to be more specific about this because some students are admitted to other degree programs in terms of performance on the same test and others on the basis of SAT scores, so that equivalent judgments must be made), .intensive interview.

Associate in Applied Science in Early Childhood Education and Social Work: Daytime program with sections for adults and with sections for recent high school graduates--high school graduation or equivalency diploma (except that an adult may have provisional admission subject to the earning of an equivalency diploma within one calendar year), satisfactory performance on adult admissions test, intensive interview.

New York University Opportunities Program: High school graduation or equivalency diploma with grades ordinarily less than 10% lower than ordinary admissions standards, intensive interview.

School of Continuing Education and Extension Services--New York University

3. Vary according to program (Johns Hopkins University)

4. High School diploma or GED, some evidence of academic ability as indicated by high school transcripts, test scores and personal interview (Columbia University, School of General Studies).

5. Successful work on 45 hours (University College of University of Richmond).

6. Must be over 25 (Rochester Institute of Technology).

7. "B" average or better in latter half of undergraduate program (Boston University-Metropolitan College).

8. Harvard University (Extension Division)

   a. With no previous college experience--must complete satisfactorily the equivalent of one year of college work--four full courses or eight half courses--under the Commission on Extension Courses, or in Har-

28

vard Summer Sch.

b. Those who have had previous college work and wish to have it evaluated for possible transfer credit must complete satisfactorily two full courses or four half-courses under the Commission on Extension Courses, or in the Harvard Summer School, before presenting official transcripts of this work.

XII. Who formulates admission policies for evening students at your institution?

A. Regular Students:
Faculty Admissions Committee
(Generally includes Director or Dean of the
Evening Division or College)   51
President's or Dean's Council   6
Dean and/or Director of the Admissions Office   23
Evening College Committee or Board and/or
Director   11
Administration and Directors   9

Other:
1. Administrative Board of the School of Continuing Education and Summer School (Washington Univ. of St. Louis)
2. State of Ohio (University of Cincinnati)
3. Dean of University College with faculty Admissions Committee and Director of Admissions (Hofstra Univ.)
4. The Administrators in the Department of Evening Classes, the Dean of Continuing Education and Administrative Council of the University (Brigham Young University)
5. The faculty of the school (New York University-- School of Continuing Education and Extension Services)
6. No Policies (University of Minnesota)
7. The college offering the courses (St. Louis University, Metropolitan College)

B. Non-degree or "special" students
Same requirements as for degree students   46
Admissions officer or registrar   12
Evening College Dean or Director   16
Administration and Directors   14
School of General Studies and Admissions Office   10

29

C. Special Degree Programs for Adults (If different
requirements for admission)
Faculty Committee   2
Admissions Officer   1

Other
1. State of Ohio (Cincinnati University)
2. Faculty of School of Continuing Education and Extension Services (New York University)
3. Dean of the Evening College (Philadelphia College of Textiles and Science)

XIII. To what extent may day and evening students enroll
in the same class?

No restrictions 70 ;   Special permission necessary 20 ;
Limited 16

Other:
1. Availability of space (University of Kentucky, Pace College)
2. No problem--only about 300 of our students are day students (University of Cincinnati)
3. Certain classes may be entered by day students only by permission of the Dean of the Evening College-- in other classes no restrictions (University of Chattanooga)
4. Day students may enroll in evening classes in the event of scheduling problems. Evening students may select day courses when full-time day students have registered (Community College of Baltimore)
5. 1/6 day vs. 5/6 evening students (Syracuse University-University College)
6. Day students enroll in evening classes for make-up to avoid scheduling conflicts and for enrichment. Evening students, transferred to night work may enroll in day classes for not more than two years (Rochester Institute of Technology)
7. At present time, half and half basis (Boston University-Metropolitan College)
8. Day students may transfer evening credit with "C" or better. Evening students normally not enrolled in day classes because basic colleges are structured for the Cooperative Plan of Education (Northeastern Univ.)
9. Of the special degree programs in our school, each

is completely day or completely evening, so there are no day or evening students in the same class. In other schools of the University with evening credit students, a full-time day student can, if it is more convenient, take one or more of his courses in the evening, but part-time students are allowed only in the evening (New York University-School of Continuing Educ. & Extension Services)
10. To the extent there is room after respective registrations (University of Bridgeport)
11. No more than 1/3 of an evening class may be populated by day division students (DePaul University)
12. First year evening student may not normally take day courses (Suffolk University)
13. All evening classes open to day students--not vice versa (The New College)
14. None--because of the military character of the Citadel.
15. This is primarily done in Library and Music classes (University of Minnesota)

In your opinion what are the advantages and/or disadvantages of the combined class with day and evening students?

Advantages:
1. The diversity of views, attitudes, and backgrounds make for greater challenge and interest   5
2. Serves to keep the "one school" concept--same standards   5
3. Chief advantages are flexibility of scheduling and and a bridging of the "generation gap". . . While both young and old sometimes feel at a disadvantage in each other's presence, the feeling soon passes   3
4. They gain greater respect for each other's role in learning that day students are not entirely theoretical in approach and that evening students are not totally dependent upon the practical approach   3
5. Combined classes mean broader course offerings-- classes will be larger and less classes cancelled due to low enrollment   8
6. Teaching is more challenging   6
7. Continuity with degree programs   4

Disadvantages
1. Possible dilution of adult level approach.
2. Only disadvantage is that frequently older students are treated the same as younger students.

31

Disadvantages of combined class with day and evening students (cont.)

3. Each group has its own regular program. They perhaps should be kept separate (except for make-up, time schedule, etc.) even though most courses are the same.
4. Disadvantages lie in age and occupational differentials primarily.
5. Disadvantage of age differences, different teaching methodology and variance in learning.
6. Very infrequently a young "matron" feels ill-at-ease at first being in the same class with students recently out of high school.
7. Day students may block some evening students from taking the course because of maximum enrollment.
8. Usually lack of experience in living on the part of the day students inhibits the use of a full potential of experience of evening students by the instructor.
9. Day students slow down evening business instructor.
10. Difficult to maintain standards in mixed classes (University of Southern California).
11. The diversity of background and interests is good, although academic performance is sometimes disappointing to day students.
12. Limits development of special adult programs.

XIV. Do you have an Orientation program for evening students?   33   73
                                                                Yes No

When is it held?
Before registration 11   First week of classes 2
Beginning of sem. (qtr.) 7   During the Semester (qtr) 4
On registration day 3

Other:
1. We have an orientation program for evening Associate in Arts and Associate in Applied Science students on an evening in the first or second week, and a daytime orientation for Associate in Applied Science in Early Childhood and Social Work students on the first day (New York University, School of Continuing Education and Extension Services)
2. One afternoon affair, Saturday or Sunday before fall and spring terms begin (St. Joseph's College)
3. Wednesday evening before first day of classes (Boston College)

4. Second week of each regular term (University of Akron) (Pace College)
5. Candidates meet faculty and staff at general open house at registration (Boston University-Metropolitan College)

XV. Additional Comments on Admissions
1. High school graduation or the equivalent is required for students who have never attended college. Well-qualified persons who are not high school graduates will be admitted upon the basis of tests. (Washington University, St. Louis)
2. Too many members of the Admissions Committee think almost exclusively in terms of the regular day student. To some degree this results in inflexibility and lack of concern for the adult part-time student. (University of Chattanooga).
3. All students are on probationary status until successful completion of 16 credits. (Loyola Evening College, Baltimore)
4. Our policy (i. e., academic units plus certain grades for degree students); high school certificate for certificates and isolated credit--does result in admission of many "probationary" status students. We believe in this for adults; we go "slow on it" for just high school graduates. (St. Joseph's College)
5. We do everything within reason to maintain evening degree programs as an integral part of the total university. (East Tennessee State University)
6. Implementation of admission standards is a function of the Evening College administration. (Johns Hopkins University)
7. Our philosophy is--those who wish to "continue to learn" should have the opportunity to do so--student a-chievement is the main "screening" device. (Wayne State University)
8. "Open-door" admissions policy--but denied admission if required background is lacking. (Dutchess Community College)
9. Since the College's programs are new (2 years), the admissions procedures and requirements are being evaluated as to effectiveness. (Boston Univeristy-Metropolitan College)
10. We have a 16 s. h. probationary program. These students are permitted to take a maximum of 16 s. h. of prescribed liberal arts courses as a basis for recon-sideration for admission. (Newark State College)

33

XV. Additional Comments on Admissions (cont.)
11. All part-time students work toward the general
Bachelor of Science degree. System of high school
grades together with matriculation after 35 q. h. of
2. 00 or better is comparable to the California State
policy. System is necessary as operation is in excess
of 12, 000 students (does not include 2500 summer students) - (Northeastern University). We have added 50
part-time academic counselors to assist students in
course selection and program planning.
12. I would like to see greater flexibility extended to the
mature and more stably motivated evening student by
Admissions Officers. Some reliable indicators should
be developed to reflect the attitudes and perseverance
levels of the adults for higher education. (Manhattan
College)
13. We do not have a separate faculty and curriculum.
Our students attend regular university classes both during the day and in the evening. Our off-campus programs are somewhat separately defined. However, for
these students permission is given for them to attend
campus classes. (The American Univ.)

II. Terminology

I. Title of your division, school or college:

A. Evening Division 19

Centenary College, C. W. Post College, Bryant College,
University of Bridgeport, Indiana Central College, Loyola University (New Orleans), Marquette University
(liberal arts), Peirce Junior College, Metropolitan College (St. Louis), Suffolk University, University of Tulsa,
Western New England College, Sir George Williams
University, Thomas More College (and Saturday Division), LaSalle College (Philadelphia), Community College of Baltimore, Northwestern University (5 divisions),
Manhattan College, Louisian State University (New Orleans).

B. Evening College 13

University of Cincinnati, Drexel Institute of Technology,
Loyola Evening College (Baltimore), St. Joseph's College, Texas Christian University, Bloomfield College,

34

Virginia Commonwealth University, Johns Hopkins University, University of Akron, University of North Carolina, Philadelphia College of Textiles and Science, American International College, Rockford College.

C. University College 12

Louisiana State University (Baton Rouge), Hofstra University, University College of Syracuse University, Rutgers University, DePaul University, University of Maryland, Drake University, Loyola University (Chicago), University of Richmond, Northeastern University, University of Southern California, University of Louisville.

D. Division of Continuing Education 10

Old Dominion College, Brigham Young University, University of Southern Mississippi, Springfield College (Mass.), University of Tampa, Babson Institute of Education, Roosevelt University, Orange County Community College, New Haven College, Ohio State University.

E. College or School of Continuing Education 6

Washington University (St. Louis), New York University (& Extension Services), East Tennessee State University, Northern Illinois University, Rochester Institute of Technology, The American University.

F. Other titles

1. Evening Class Program (non-degree) - University of Kentucky.
2. The Evening and Special Classes Division of the University - University of Chattanooga.
3. Division of University Extension - University of Illinois, University of Tennessee (Knoxville), Harvard University, University of Windsor, University of Toronto.
4. Evening and General Studies Division - Queensborough Community College.
5. Evening School - McNeese State College.
6. School of General Studies - Brooklyn College of City University of New York, Columbia University, City College of New York.
7. Adult Education & Evening School (Millikin University).

F. Other titles (cont.)
   8. Department of Evening Classes - University of
      Minnesota.
   9. Evening College of Arts, Sciences and Business
      Administration (Boston College).
  10. The Citadel Evening Program - The Citadel.
  11. Division of Special Programs - Miami-Dade Junior
      College.
  12. Evening Program and Continuing Education - Roan-
      oke College, Bronx Community College.
  13. Evening session - St. Bonaventure University;
      Polytech Institute of Brooklyn; St. Francis College.
  14. Division of Business Administration - Iona College.
  15. Office of Continuing Education - University of Den-
      ver; Dutchess Community College.
  16. Department of Continuing Education - Washburn
      University.
  17. School of Continuing Studies - College of William
      and Mary.
  18. Continuing Adult Education and Community Services
      - Northern Virginia Community College.
  19. Division of Field Service - Trenton State Univer-
      sity; Newark State College.
  20. University Continuing Education Division - Cleve-
      land College of Case Western Reserve University.
  21. Adult Education Division - Drury College.
  22. Extra-sessional Credit - University of British
      Columbia.
  23. Metropolitan College - Boston University.
  24. No special designation. Each school offers day
      and evening programs. The School of Continuing
      Education is intended for non-matriculating and spe-
      cial students - Pace College; Purdue University,
      (Calumet Campus).
  25. Center for Continuing Education - University of
      Georgia.

II. How would you define the meaning of this term as used
    in your institution?

   A. Evening Division
      1. Ours is a regular part of our college, and that
         means just that it is the evening program of the
         college. We do experiment more in this division
         than in the Day school (Centenary College of Louisi-
         ana).

36

2. Regular collegiate degree-oriented programs offered in the evening (LaSalle College).
3. Comprises all adult undergraduate students enrolled at C. W. Post College and at its extension. It also includes all non-credit continuing education programs (C. W. Post College).
4. Responsible for adult education, degree and non-credit (special) courses, evening and Saturday classes - on and off-campus - Bryant College.
5. As a Division of the University (University of Bridgeport).
6. It is an administrative term to distinguish between the day and evening programs (Indiana Central College).
7. Originally, it was a Division of Arts & Sciences; now for practical purposes it is autonomous (Loyola University - New Orleans).
8. A semi-autonomous division of the day college (Marquette University).
9. Each of the five day divisions is academically responsible for its own evening programs which are identical to its day program leading to a degree (Northwestern University).
10. The evening division at Manhattan College is an integral unit of the College. Its primary purpose is identical with the objectives of the college. The division is a separate academic unit under its own director, which presently awards the BBA degree and AAS degree (Manhattan College).

B. Evening College

1. We offer our own courses and bachelor degrees, control faculty, have identical status with other campus colleges. We offer our own non-credit work (University of Cincinnati).
2. Completely autonomous undergraduate program of studies offered after 6 P. M. (Drexel Institute of Technology).
3. Programs similar to day, but offered in evening hours usually to fully employed older students (Loyola Evening College - Baltimore).
4. We are a degree-granting liberal arts college - evening and part-time. (The evening is not 100% accurate; nor is the "part-time") - (St. Joseph's College).
5. A separate administration, operating much as a sec-

B. Evening College (cont.)

    ond shift would do in industry (Virginia Commonwealth University).

  6. A program of part-time higher education for adults. Emphasis is placed on work toward certificates and degrees (Johns Hopkins University).

  7. A general two-year program for adult students (University of North Carolina).

C. University College

  1. Defined as a part-time college (Louisiana State University - Baton Rouge).

  2. It is the Continuing Education Division of the University (University College of Syracuse University).

  3. A college within the framework of the University (Rutgers University).

  4. A service-oriented administrative unit facilitating the continuing education responsibilities of the university which also grants a degree (University of Maryland).

  5. Programs and courses for adults (De Paul University).

  6. University college is one of nine colleges which offers evening, Saturday and extension classes. The Center for Continuing Education develops programs for business, industry, community service, and other groups of a non-credit nature (Drake University).

  7. The part-time degree-granting division which offers classes in the late afternoon, evening and on Saturday (Loyola University - Chicago).

  8. University College, so-called because it draws upon the resources of the other colleges of the university, offers part-time programs in Liberal Arts, Business Administration, Law Enforcement and Security and Health-Related programs, leading to the Associate in Science and Bachelor of Science degrees. Workshops and seminars are offered for degree credit... the university college provides curricula which cut across traditional subject-matter areas to meet the particular needs of adult students (Northeastern University).

D. Division of Continuing Education

  1. Division in charge of resident, evening program, extension program, public services and summer session (Old Dominion College).

2. The administrative unit responsible for all credit and non-credit programs over and above those administered by day deans of the University (University of Southern Mississippi).

3. The Dean of the Division of Continuing Education administers campus credit courses for non-full time day students (Brigham Young University).

4. Continuing education basically represents the opportunity for adults to earn their undergraduate degree on a part-time basis. It also includes non-credit institutes, conferences, workshops and extension courses (Springfield College - Massachusetts).

5. Offers courses for credit or non-credit (as the student qualifies, or if the materials are of college level). Courses open with above restrictions to all the community (University of Tampa).

6. Credit and non-credit courses offered outside regular day hours - off-campus courses - seminars and institutes (Babson Institute, Business Administration).

E. College or School of Continuing Education

1. We have no expectation that the confusion of terminology will be ended and so have used this rather long and clumsy name as a general way of indicating that considerable range of activities will be found here that are found in other institutions that are called university colleges, colleges of adult education, evening colleges, extension divisions, etc. ... as well as other activities that are not to be found in other institutions (School of Continuing Education and Extension Services of New York University).

2. Includes evening degree and certificate credit courses; also conferences, lectures, and other continuing activities of a general nature. Includes some continuing professional education (Washington University - St. Louis).

3. A division through which educational services of the university are extended to individuals and groups other than day students. Includes both credit and non-credit programs. (East Tennessee State University).

4. Any program not part of the day programs except where NSF grant is involved. Also includes day programs in the summer session (Rochester Institute of Technology).

39

E. College or School of Continuing Education (cont.)

    5. A college designed to act as a link between the adult student and the university. CCE enables the adult student to make maximum use of university facilities (The American University).

    6. Evening Division - Part-time evening students on campus (Northern Illinois University).

F. Other

    1. Division of Continuing Studies - functions to service the needs of students who do not choose to make college work a full-time objective (Memphis State University).

    2. Evening Class Program - Non-degree students meeting after 5 P. M. (University of Kentucky).

    3. School of General Studies - primary objective is to offer higher educational opportunities to working men and women (Brooklyn College of City University of New York).

    4. Division of Special Programs - evening, week-ends and off-campus classes (Miami-Dade Junior College).

    5. Evening Program and Continuing Education - This office takes care of evening classes. The Continuing Education was added to take care of non-credit activities, institutes, conferences, and business and industrial education (Roanoke College).

    6. University Extension - The extension program includes courses in the three areas of Humanities, Natural Sciences and Social Sciences (Harvard University Extension Division).

    7. Division of Business Administration - We offer the B. B. A. Degree in the evening (Iona College).

    8. Extra-Sessional Credit - Regular university courses for the student pursuing his degree by part-time, scheduled at times most convenient for this student (University of British Columbia).

    9. Office of Continuing Education - Educational opportunities for area residents whose daily responsibilities prevent them from attending the College's day division as full-time students and who seek to complete initial higher educational objectives, up-date skills and techniques, and seek cultural enrichment (Dutchess Community College).

   10. Center for Continuing Education - includes both credit and non-credit courses offered to adults whose

primary occupation is other than that of full-time college students. (University of Georgia)

III. Many college and university administrators think of Continuing Education as series of non-credit courses, conferences, and institutes. How would you define Continuing Education? (A limited number of definitions are listed below)

1. Continuing education would include credit activities as well as non-credit courses, conferences and institutes (Washington University - St. Louis).
2. Continuing education means the continuation of education whether it be through credit courses or non-credit programs, conferences and institutes or combination of these (University of Chattanooga).
3. Any educational activity which follows the point at which the individual had considered his education terminal and which he pursues as an adult. An adult may be defined as anyone over 16 or who has completed high school (Rochester Institute of Technology).
4. A program which allows the intellectually qualified high school graduate of any age to enroll in part or full-time study which may or may not lead to a degree (Cleveland College of Case Western Reserve University).
5. Any process by which men and women (either alone or in groups) try to improve themselves by increasing their skill, their knowledge, or their sensitivity; or the process by which individuals or organizations try to improve men and women in these ways (Cy Houle) - (University of Illinois).
6. A course, conference, institute and/or workshop designed to keep a college graduate abreast of the developments in the field of his interest or a related field (Drexel Institute of Technology).
7. Credit courses day and evening, non-credit courses, conferences, institutes, theater programming, publications, radio, TV, etc. which focus on the part-time student and adult (University College of Syracuse University).
8. Continuing Education is a series of learning situations aimed at solving problems recognized by the learner as needing solutions. This includes both formal and informal experiences moving a person from where he is in the direction of some desired goal. (Drake University).

41

Definition of Continuing Education (cont.)

9. All experiences which enrich the quality of the individuals' thought, performance and perspective is appropriate to our notion of Continuing Education. (The New School)

10. The provision of a means for the continued pursuit of learning--via non-degree, degree and non-credit. (The American University).

11. It is an educational service provided for adults who are seeking to improve themselves personally and professionally in order to keep abreast of the world in which they live and live richer and fuller lives. (University of Georgia).

III. Fees

I. Is there a fee differential between day and evening classes?

$\dfrac{51}{\text{Yes}}$ $\dfrac{53}{\text{No}}$

II. If so, what is the justification?
   1. Day students have services and facilities not available to evening students _15_.
   2. The overhead is not quite as extensive and we have paid the Evening Division faculty lower salaries.
   3. Teachers are, for the most part, part-time; evening students do not enjoy the fringe benefits of day students.
   4. The cost of day instruction is greater.
   5. Evening classes in our institution have higher tuition rates-evening classes are financially, self-supporting (University of Kentucky, Trenton State College, Newark State College).
   6. Amortization of capital investment not charged against Evening College (Drexel Institute of Technology).
   7. Competition in the evening with other institutions _6_.

Examples of Comparative Day & Evening Tuition

Part-time Day	Part-time Evening	School
1. $40 per sem. hr.	$35 per sem. hr.	Centenary College
2. $1400 (full-time)	$30 per hr.	LaSalle College
3. $80 per hr.	$40 per hr.	Washington Univ. (St. Louis)

42

Part-time Day	Part-time Evening	School
4. $12.50 per hr.	$14 per hr.	Univ. of Kentucky
5. $40 per sem. hr.	$30 per sem. hr.	Univ. of Chattanooga
6. "Range" scale	$15 per sem. hr.	Univ. of Illinois
7. $45 per hr. &	Institution fee &	
Inst. fee	$25	Drexel Inst. of Tech.
8. $50 per sem. hr.	$22 per sem. hr.	Loyola Univ.
		(New Orleans)
9. ----	$13 per sem. hr.	Univ. of Minnesota
10. $45 per sem. hr.	$16.67 per sem. hr.	Bryant College
11. $80 per sem. hr.	$30 per sem. hr.	Johns Hopkins Univ.
12. $53 hr.	$37 hr.	Metropolitan Coll.
		(St. Louis)

III. What are your refund policies?

1.	Percentage refund within first week only	7
2.	Percentage refund within two weeks	13
3.	Percentage refund within three weeks	11
4.	Percentage refund within four weeks	11
5.	Percentage refund within five weeks	15
6.	Percentage refund within six weeks	6
7.	Percentage refund within seven weeks	1
8.	Percentage refund within eight weeks	7
9.	Percentage refund within nine weeks	2
10.	Percentage refund 1/3 or 1/2 of term	4
11.	No refund after classes begin	4
12.	No other policies or listed as "same as for day students"	20

Examples of Refund Policies:

1. No refund after the beginning of the second week of class.
2. First two weeks - 80%; second two weeks - 60%; third two weeks - 40%; fourth two weeks - 20%   4
3. First week - 90%; two weeks - 80%; three weeks - 70%; four weeks - 50%; five weeks - 30%; six weeks - 10%.
4. 10% of charges are refunded for each week up to tenth week.
5. Generally full refund.
6. If a student withdraws after the beginning of a class, he forfeits 12.5% of his fees for each 1/6 of the class offered to date.   No refund is given after the middle of the course.

43

Examples of Refund Policies (cont.)

7. First five days of classes - 100%; five to ten days - 50%; after - 0%.
8. No refunds once classes have begun.
9. Full reimbursement up to third week of classes, none later.
10. a) Mail registrants who withdraw prior to regular registration receive full refund minus $5 processing fee;
    b) Withdrawal prior to deadline (second week) may receive 75% refund. No refund later.
11. Drop within two weeks - 25% refund.
12. No refund after first week of classes.
13. First week - 100%; second week - 60%; third week - 40%; fourth week - 20%.
14. 100% before classes; 60% during first 1/3 of term; 30% to first 1/2 of term.

IV. Faculty and Faculty Recruitment

I. Do you have a policy regarding the percentage of faculty for evening classes that are full-time faculty members?

20	85
Yes	No

Approximately what percentage are full-time?

15	26	21	14	26
0 - 24%	25 - 40%	45 - 60%	65 - 80%	85 - 100%

II. Recruitment
A. Who has the final authority for hiring full and/or part-time faculty members for evening classes in your institution?

Full-time		Part-time	
Dean and/or Director	37	Dean or Director of Evening	
President or Chancellor	5	Division or College	12
Vice-President for Academic Affairs	4	Same as for full-time faculty	90
Department chairmen	27		
Both the Chairmen and Dean or Director	14		
Dean of Day College	14		
Committee on Faculty Apts.	2		

44

B. Can you as Director of the evening division or college, reject a faculty member who has been assigned to teach evening classes? $\underline{\quad 67 \quad}$ $\underline{\quad 30 \quad}$
                                    Yes   No

C. Do you employ any full-time faculty members who teach exclusively in the evening? $\underline{\quad 31 \quad}$ $\underline{\quad 76 \quad}$
                                                     Yes   No

Schools employing full-time faculty members in the evening

1. LaSalle College (2 only)
2. University of Illinois
3. Old Dominion College
4. Brooklyn College of City Univ. of N. Y.
5. Drake University (College of Business - 20%)
6. Cleveland Coll. of Case Western Reserve Univ.
7. Drury College
8. Loyola Evening College (Baltimore)
9. St. Joseph's College
10. Rutgers University
11. Loyola University (New Orleans)
12. Manhattan College
13. Pace College
14. New York University (School of Continuing Educ.)
15. Bronx Community College
16. University of Minnesota
17. C. W. Post College
18. Rockford College
19. City College of New York (42)
20. University of Southern Mississippi
21. University of Bridgeport
22. DePaul University
23. University of Maryland
24. East Tennessee State University
25. University of Richmond (Evening College)
26. University of Tennessee (Knoxville)
27. Queensborough Community College
28. Rochester Institute of Technology
29. Drexel Institute of Technology

If so, are they responsible to you as Director or Dean of the evening division or College?

$\underline{\quad 20 \quad}$ $\underline{\quad 5 \quad}$ $\underline{\quad 5 \quad}$
Yes   No   Partially

D. Can you as evening Director (or Dean) engage an instructor without the consent of the department head if this person refuses to staff these classes?

48	37	10
Yes	No	Would prefer not to

E. Do you hold regular faculty meetings with your evening faculty?

46	56
Yes	No

If so, when are they held?
1. Once each semester or quarter   24
2. Once a year   13
3. Before classes begin   5
4. First week of classes   1

Other

1. Dinner meetings (LaSalle College)
2. As appropriate (University of Illinois, Roosevelt University, University of Cincinnati)
3. Late afternoons (University of Toronto)
4. Four times a year (School of Continuing Education & Extension Services - New York University)
5. First night of classes each evening (Roanoke Coll.)
6. Twice a month (afternoons) (University of Bridgeport, University of Richmond)
7. Regular evenings (Wayne State University, Dutchess Community College)

F. What are your policies regarding regular faculty members teaching credit or non-credit courses or participating in institutes, seminars and conferences as an overload?

21	64	3	15
No overload	Permitted	Occasionally	Restricted

Amount of overload permitted:

1. Limit of three (or four) semester hours (or one overload class) per semester (Quarter)   28
2. Limit of eight semester hours per year beyond normal schedule   3
3. Two nights a week (six semester hours) in evening division   2
4. Consent of Academic Dean or Department Head   10
5. One overload class allowed each year   2

46

6. Amount received cannot exceed 20% of
   regular salary   1
7. Six hours of credit may be taught as an overload each year   3
8. Limited to no more than one day a week consulting, interpreted to mean a maximum of two
   evenings a week teaching--three periods an evening.   1
9. As overload, we pay $500 per three semester
   hour course--if they teach at night as part of
   their regular load, they are not paid extra   1
10. They receive extra compensation by academic
    rank   22
11. Full-time faculty members are allowed one
    course overload in Extension   1

V. Scheduling

I. Are you, as Dean or Director, responsible for the evening class schedule in your institution? 85   19
                                              Yes   No

II. If not, who is responsible?

   A. Registrar   4
   B. Department Heads   5
   C. University Administration   4
   D. Day Deans   2

III. What is the procedure for compiling the evening class
     schedule in your college or university?

   1. Department heads (or schools) submit evening
      class schedule for approval by the Dean or Di-
      rector who may make revisions.   43
   2. Schedule is based on the needs of the students
      and requirements of the curricula.   14
   3. The registrar requests schedules--submits to
      evening division or University College for ap-
      proval.   9
   4. The evening class schedule is planned by the
      Director(s) or Dean of The Evening College
      and then it is submitted to departments for
      staffing and/or approval.   18
   5. Courses are scheduled in cycles over the years
      to enable adults to meet degree requirements--

Procedure for compiling evening class schedule (cont.)

schedule is revised only when necessary.   6
6. Past schedules are carefully checked to see what
   courses materialized and what courses are needed
   to meet the curricula requirements and student
   needs.   10

Remarks

1. An attempt is made to regularly cycle some offerings so
   as to permit the earning of a degree through evening
   classes (Marquette University).
2. Our program administrator or department head turns in
   "room cards" requesting space for his classes and sections of classes at the same time that he turns in bulletin copy. This "schedule" is subject to revision through
   negotiations between my office and the program administrator when space is not available either inside the university or in rented space outside. The availability of
   classrooms inside the university is a complex problem
   because of the number of schools using the same build-
   ings. As a consequence, over the years, basically a
   "Quota" system has developed so that a school can expect
   to have for a semester the same number of rooms at the
   same time that it had one year before. (School of Continuing Education and Extension Services of New York University).
3. It is prepared by the Director in March and submitted
   to the faculty and students for suggestions. (Loyola University, New Orleans)
4. The schedule is constructed with regard to previous experience, anticipated student demand, staffing considera-
   tions, course sequence, facility availability, etc. We
   make an effort to balance evenings and periods to facili-
   tate student movement. (Johns Hopkins University)
5. Offerings come to the Director of the Evening Session
   through the Deans and Registrar. He makes up the final
   schedule. (St. Bonaventure University)
6. A matrix system is used to spread "core" and "required"
   courses over the evening. (University of Richmond)
7. The schedule has evolved over many years and is revised
   only insofar as necessary to make it possible for degree
   or diploma students to schedule their classes on the most
   convenient nights (Rochester Inst. of Tech.).
8. The Registrar requests schedule for the entire year, both
   day and evening. The evening schedule is then sent to
   University College. While the original schedule is com-

piled by the department chairmen, it is subject to approval by the Dean. (Hofstra University)

9. College catalog made up in February or March before the coming academic year. The schedule for fall courses is made up then and printed with the catalog, distributed in April or May. Therefore, we need six months or more for a new course or a change of course--and a change in the schedule. (St. Joseph's College)

10. Area program administrators do initial work in consultation with other deans and department chairmen-- schedule is assembled by Director of Evening Classes Division. (University College of Syracuse University).

IV. Do you as Dean or Director have the authority to revise or make additions to the evening class schedule?

80	11	12
Yes	No	With consultation

V. Are your three-hour classes scheduled one night __21__ two nights __16__ or both __30__ each week?
In your opinion, which is preferable? __20__,
one night

22	20
two nights	both, depending on subject

VI. Research

The Research Committee of AUEC is interested in any research projects in adult education which have been completed, are in progress or are planned for the near future. Do you have any research projects completed or in progress at your institution?

24	70
Yes	No

School	Topic
1. LaSalle College	1. Only statistical materials relative to our own situation in academic performance, retention, withdrawals, etc.
2. Washington Univ. (St. Louis)	2. Available later in the year.
3. Univ. of Cincinnati	3. Ph. D. thesis--Gail Nelcamp

49

School	Topic

4. Hofstra Univ.

5. Brooklyn College

6. Brigham Young University

7. St. Joseph's College

8. Univ. College of Syracuse Univ.

9. Marquette Univ.

10. New York Univ. -- School of Continuing Education and Extension Services

4. Study on correlation between admission advisement test and student achievement is planned.

5. We regularly conduct the variety of institutional research projects.

6. A survey was made in 1964 regarding our evening students.

7. There is a continuing study on admissions--to find out if the adult, or the younger student, according to, or in spite of, his high school grades does better in evening college. Remember, we accept on the high school record. Results so far continue to indicate that the age of the student, i. e., the number of years out of high school, is a better presage of his success than recent graduation.

8. One staff member is about to do a doctoral dissertation on the attitude of faculty toward Continuing Education.

9. Doctoral dissertation underway which will explore the desirability and feasibility of offering unique adult degree programs at Marquette University.

10. "A History of the Division of General Education, New York University--1934-1959"--Ed. D. Thesis submitted by Anne Freidus
"Patterns of Educational Use of a Televised Public Affairs Program --A Study of METROPOLIS: Creator or Destroyer"--sponsored by the University Council on Education for Public Responsibility. Study Director: Harry L. Miller
"New York University's Harlem Seminars"--a narrative account of a Title I (Higher Education Act of 1965) project under the direction of Harry L. Miller.
"Survey of University Adult Education in the Metropolitan Area of New

School	Topic

New York" A study made possible by a grant from the Fund for the Advancement of Education, The Ford Foundation under the direction of Mrs. Caroline Ellwood. "An Evaluation of the MIND Adult Education Center of West 114th St. in Harlem" An evaluation of a novel attempt at prevocational basic education for residents of 114th Street between 7th and 8th Avenues by MIND, Inc., a subsidiary of Corn Products Corporation.

11. DePaul Univ.   11. Various ad hoc committees are constantly being appointed to research particular phases of adult education.

12. Drake Univ.   12. A study of students registered in the fall of 1967 who did not continue in the spring of 1968 was undertaken.

13. Nassau Community College   13. Cooperative Opportunity in Public Education (COPE).

14. Virginia Commonwealth Univ.   14. We make simple studies from time to time usually with reference to students in the Evening College and Summer School Classes.

15. East Tennessee State Coll.   15. We plan to conduct a study comparing day and evening classes for procedures and results.

16. Suffolk Univ.   16. The Associate Dean of the Evening Division is presently conducting a long-range Planning Study that includes both day and evening divisions.

17. New Haven College   17. Survey in Groton and Waterbury area for additional course requests in our already existing extensions.

18. The American Univ.   18. Various projects through our Labor Studies Center.

19. Univ. of Denver   19. The Office of Continuing Education at the University of Denver plans to cooperate with other schools in the Denver area on a project sponsored by the Adult Education Council of Metropolitan Denver which obtains information on enrollment trends.

20. Univ. of Southern California   20. We envision some studies on the use of TV in achieving economy efficien-

School	Topic
	cy relating goals and in teacher education and in extending off-campus "in-plant."
21. City College of New York	21. We are anxious to hear about "attitude" and "motivation" tests. Motivation seems to be a very important factor in determining success. High school average and "aptitude" tests do not predict well enough.
22. Orange County Community Coll.	22. A five year prediction of Continuing Education Programs at Orange County Community College.
23. Thomas More College	23. Completed a minimal Level Research Study for high attrition rates among Evening and Saturday Division Students.
24. Case Western Reserve Univ.	24. We are researching the mature woman student who has returned to the classroom after an absence of several years. We are also researching the "Dismissed" students to determining failure factors.
25. Indiana Central College	25. A study of the relationship between the Advanced Test of the Graduate Record Examination and the undergraduate index for predicting graduate index.

26. Drury College   26-29. - No topics listed.
27. Univ. of North Carolina
28. Newark State College
29. Univ. of Tennessee (Knoxville)

VII. How do you compare your day and evening classes in terms of quality?

78	18	10
Equal	Equal or better	More variability

VIII. Are your part-time evening students eligible for the Dean's List?

53	50
Yes	No

If so, how many hours are required for eligibility?

Dean's List:

School	Hours Required	Grade Point Average
1. Univ. of Cincinnati	6 credits	3.50
2. Bloomfield College	6 sem. hrs.	3.20 honors, 3.60 high honors
3. Drexel Inst. of Tech.	6.5 qtr. hrs.	3.50
4. Manhattan College	8 credits	3.00
5. St. Francis College	8 hrs.	3.00
6. Thomas More College	8 cr. hrs.	3.50 (separate Director's List)
7. Drury College	8 hrs.	3.30
8. Loyola Univ. (New Orleans)	9 hrs.	3.00
9. Loyola Evening Coll. (Baltimore)	9 sem. hrs.	"B" avg. in all courses
10. Boston College	9 hrs.	82% or above
11. Suffolk Univ.	9 hrs.	3.00
12. Columbia Univ. -Sch. of Gen. Studies	9 pts in 3 Lib. Arts subjects	3.10
13. Philadelphia Coll. of Textiles and Science	9 hrs.	3.33
14. Hofstra Univ.	12 cr. for yr.	3.30 (Honors List for part-time students)
15. Rutgers Univ. (Univ. Coll)	12 hrs.	1.90
16. Peirce Junior Coll.	12 sem. hrs.	3.50
17. Nassau Comm. Coll.	12 hrs.per yr.	3.25
18. Washburn Univ. of Topeka	12 hrs.	2.00
19. Univ. of Tennessee (Knoxville)	12 hrs.	3.00
20. Polytech Inst. of Brooklyn	12 cr. per yr.	3.00 (separate list for evening)
21. Rochester Inst. of Tech.	12 hrs. per yr.	3.20
22. Cleveland Coll. of Case Western Res. Univ.	15 hrs.	3.00
23. St. Joseph's College	30 credits	"B" avg. in term
24. Old Dominion Coll. (Honor Soc.)	18 hrs.	3.50
25. Univ. of Maryland	15 sem. hrs.	3.50
26. Brigham Young Univ.	45 hrs. (Magna cum laude, cum laude)	3.80 Magna cum laude; 3.50-3.79-cum laude
27. Univ. of S. Calif. (Univ. Coll.)	Varies by schools	
28. Sir George Williams Univ.	30 sem. hrs. (no "F's")	3.00

Dean's List (cont.)

School	Hours Required	Grade Point Average
29. Univ. of So. Mississippi	15 qtr. hrs.	3.25
30. City College of New York	32hrs. or more	3.20
31. LaSalle College	33 hrs.	3.40
32. American Int. College	6 cr. or 9 cr.	4.00 or 3.00, respectively

VI. General

I. Is your institution participating in any of the following innovative practices?

A. Offering credit and/or non-credit courses in "store front" locations off-campus for economically deprived populations? <u>17</u> <u>90</u>
   Yes No

Courses and Programs

1. We are about to offer some non-credit courses in this area. (University of Cincinnati)
2. Several proposals pending. (University of Illinois)
3. Informal tutorial work is done. (Loyola Evening College, Baltimore)
4. Yes, if you mean this broadly as in the ghetto or appropriate location. (Univ. College of Syracuse University).
5. Offering tutorial and remedial programs on campus. (Rutgers University)
6. One of the reports submitted describes an attempt at non-credit courses for economically deprived students in off-campus locations. These courses worked out fairly well, but it was difficult to see which way to follow this up as satisfactorily as we had been able to follow up offering on-campus special courses. (School of Continuing Education and Extension Services-University of New York)
7. No, however, we are doing a big job in libraries and schools. (C.W. Post College)
8. Now in the planning stages with A.I.C. (Bryant College)
9. Under discussion. (Miami-Dade Junior College)
10. We do have scholarship assistance for those who can handle our regular program. (Suffolk University)
11. Head Start and Upward Bound Programs. (Roanoke College)

12. A tutorial project staffed by volunteer tutors (for mostly college students) and operating 10 ghetto locations--is partially administered by the Evening College. This is an O. E. O. funded project. Students being tutored are elementary and secondary school students. (University of Akron)
13. Special tutorial projects, Social Action Institutes, Urban Semester programs, and Medical program in Watts. (University College of the University of Southern California)
14. Once a year 40 students are selected at random from those anticipating graduation in the next 12-18 months. (Rockford College)
15. Four major off-campus locations, and use a collegiate bus. (Orange County Community College)
16. Non-credit courses offered in converted elementary school in urban area. (Thomas More College)
17. We are currently offering tutorial services to failing students. (Community College of Baltimore)

B. To what extent do students at your institution participate in any discussions regarding academic program?

29	29	42
Considerably	Limited	No participation

How do they participate?

1. Students are included on the Academic Affairs Committee, Curriculum Committee, or Senate and/or on many of the major standing committees of the faculty.   25
2. Through extensive questionnaires, surveys and individual conferences.   3
3. Through Evening Students' Honor Society.   2
4. Representation on Continuing Education or Evening Division Committee or Council (policy-making)   6
5. Student-faculty Relations Committee discusses academic programs.   3
6. Students have Academic Affairs Committee.   3
7. Student participation under consideration by faculty.   3

Individual responses

1. Student members participate along with day faculty and evening administrators in the Committee on Academic Policy. (Washington University, St. Louis)
2. Unable to organize an Evening College student government which would be representative of the student body.

55

Individual responses (cont.)
At present, the Evening College Honors Society at its
regularly scheduled meetings provides this liaison.
(Old Dominion College)
3. Student Council (evening students) now in operation ten
years. College (day) has campus-wide discussions this
year. (St. Joseph's College)
4. The student senate sponsors teacher's evaluation questionnaire. The President of all student organizations,
senators and other student leaders meet monthly with
the President, Dean of Students, Dean of Continuing
Education, etc., for a dinner meeting and discuss
school problems. (University of Tulsa)
5. We always encourage student reactions to programs students desire. We conduct student surveys from time
to time on various questions. (Johns Hopkins University)
6. Candidates for graduation make suggestions for future
evening schedule. (Loyola University, New Orleans)
7. In short order, we should have two students on our Committee on Instruction--the policy board for curriculum.
(Columbia University)
8. We do have a student-faculty Relations Committee made
up of matriculated and non-matriculated students and
full and part-time faculty. Several ad hoc committees
of the standing committee are examining the academic
programs. (Manhattan College)

C. What other innovative practices are used at your institution?

1. Those determined through meetings with students (forum
hours) and instructors. (LaSalle College)
2. Special non-credit programs and electronic-media.
(University of Illinois)
3. a. University scholarships for part-time students.
b. Scholarships for Negro adult students. (Hofstra University)
c. Credit by examination.
4. College-for-a-day program for adults (Hofstra University)
5. Much emphasis on leadership development through co-
curricular and extra-curricular activities (Drexel Institute of Technology)
6. a. Faculty participation for part-time faculty. Although
formal votes in our faculty meetings must, according to the University by-laws that control all of the

faculties, be restricted to full-time faculty with...
rank, all part-time faculty are invited to faculty
meetings and may otherwise hold offices in the
faculty.

b. The various programs have appointed or elected faculty "ombudsmen" to whom the student can, anonymously and without prejudice, bring complaints or problems. Similarly, there is a faculty ombudsman for full-time faculty and also one for part-time faculty.

c. A Newsletter (Continuing Education) is published eight times a year for circulation to faculty and students.

d. A "house organ" called "School Notes" is circulated at irregular intervals to administrators and office staff of the school. Mailing list: 172.

e. "Library Notes" --reviews of significant books or articles--is circulated at irregular intervals to administrators and full-time faculty.

f. A Program of Special Events--lectures, musical or dance performances, colloquia, art film discussions, poetry readings, happenings--is announced through the Newsletter, in the University "house organ" mailed to all administrators and faculty, and in the city newspapers and on radio stations. During the current year, this will mean that approximately 50 events will be open to faculty and students of our School, other schools of the University, and to the general public, without charge. (School of Continuing Education & Extension Service, New York University)

7. Evening College faculty professional committee sponsors seminars for full and part-time faculty concerned with various aspects of increasing effectiveness. (Texas Christian University)

8. On the College Council (supreme body, under the President and Trustees) are four students (two from day college, two from evening college); 20 students sit on the general college assembly (10 day and 10 evening). (St. Joseph's College)

9. a.] Intersession Summer Programs, June 10-July 10;
b.] Black history and Sociology problems taught by Negro scholars; c.] Projected degree programs for adults; d.] Projected cooperation with independent Continuing Education projects in Southern California in noncredit liberal arts discussion programs; e.] Television education--public relations programs; f.] Excellence in Teaching Awards Programs; g.] Numerous special conferences and institutes; h.] Overseas programs for

Innovative practices (cont.)

  regular students and military persons and dependents;
  i.] Alumni Continuing Education programs. (University
  College of the University of Southern California)
10. Special mini-grants up to $200 are available to any in-
  structor who has some teaching innovation he wishes
  to try. (University of Tennessee, Knoxville)
11. "Two Platoon System"--use of classrooms for two
  courses in evening. (Northeastern University)
12. Use schedule block courses during the daytime in our
  Women's Program, etc. (Orange County Community
  College)
13. Evening Division newspaper, summer session informals
  for the faculty and students. (Newark State College)
14. Day program degree totally by examination--no credits
  or grades. (The New School)
15. Special and new credit degrees: Urban Affairs (Undergraduate & graduate), Master of Liberal Studies.
  (Boston University-Metropolitan College)
16. LTV courses for credit on commercial stations. Residential center 90 miles from campus. (Drury College)
17. We have just introduced a new Freshmen Studies Program. (Cleveland College of Case Western Reserve
  University)
18. We are just beginning to use closed circuit TV, both
  day and evening. We have an IBM 1500 Computer a-
  vailable to all, but specifically for students of the National Tech. Inst. for the Deaf. (Rochester Institute of
  Technology)
19. Extension center at Fort Polk. (McNeese State College,
  Louisiana)
20. Honors students may participate in non-credit courses.
  (University of Toledo)
21. Our program is essentially one offering credit courses
  to be applied toward degrees and certificates. We are
  moving heavily into the area of graduate degrees and
  work because we feel that this is the area where we
  can make the greatest contribution in our geographic
  area. (Johns Hopkins University)
22. Five classes by educational television--from 500 to 600
  adult students attending classes on Saturday mornings,
  a few drive in and take Friday night class also). (Virginia Commonwealth University)
23. Have joint program at Kingsport involving the University
  of Tennessee. (East Tennessee State University)
24. We are expanding Committee participation, plan weekly
  open meetings with President, Vice-President and de-

partment Chairmen. (University of Tampa)

25. Interdisciplinary Senior Honors Program; also students are placed in Social Work Agencies as part of Field experience work. (Suffolk University)

26. Open House Workshops for Library administrators; day classes designed for adults. (Springfield College, Mass.)

27. Calculus and Physics studied together for half a night each, twice a week. (Western New England College)

28. We have recently initiated a Developmental Studies Program (both remedial and tutorial) for college students from disadvantaged backgrounds who have had or who are anticipating academic difficulty. (University of Akron)

29. Law students are participating as recorders and advisers for Model City residents' committees. (University of Denver)

30. Older matriculated students are counselling the younger matriculated and non-matriculated students on academic, job and personal related problems. (Manhattan College)

31. Off-campus and Saturday classes for Law Enforcement personnel. (Bryant College)

32. Masters degree program in the area of Liberal Arts offered in the evening. (Indiana Central College)

33. Numerous community oriented programs have been conducted. (DePaul University)

34. We have a weekly television "Junior College Forum" which from time to time features the Division of Special Programs. (Miami-Dade Junior College)

35. Eight-week terms at military centers. (University of Maryland)

36. Model Cities Leadership, New Careers with deferred credit and Art for Deprived Children conducted in neighborhood centers. (Drake University)

II. In general, do you feel that your evening division is receiving adequate support (in terms of adequate stress and financial support) in comparison with the day program? <u>62</u>   <u>38</u>   <u>7</u>
       Yes   No Limited

Does your administration recognize the need and the importance of your adult education program? <u>80</u>   <u>26</u>
                        Yes   No

Comments

1. In a small liberal arts college, funds are limited.

Comments (cont.)

2. Almost all of the emphasis is placed on the day program. I fear that I have not been able to impress certain top administrators with the importance of the program.
3. The Board of Trustees is especially interested in the program.
4. Higher salaries for part-time instructors will help, but college funds are inadequate.
5. There are some areas in which we could use more support. We need more administrative service offices open during evenings for students.
6. The administration recognizes--the faculty "no."
7. Our President advocates 1) Scholarship, 2) research, 3) community service, as major roles of the University. The latter, of course, is primarily our operation.

III. To whom are you as Director or Dean of the Evening Division, school or college, responsible?

President or Chancellor	28
Dean of Academic Affairs, Academic Vice-President or Provost	44
Vice-President or Vice-Chancellor of the Univ.	6
Dean of the College	4
Dean of Instruction or of the Faculty	5

Other:

1. Dean or Director of University Extension	5
2. Dean of Continuing Education	2
3. Vice-President of Continuing Education	1
4. Dean of Humanities	2
5. Dean of A & S or Liberal Arts	3
6. Vice-Pres. for Regional Campus Adm.	1

IV. What audio-visual and other technical instructional aids are used in your division or college of Continuing Education?

Most all schools have the usual audio-visual aids available for evening instruction. A few schools have closed-circuit television, various projectors are used. Two schools have unusual facilities and programs:

1. New York University--School of Continuing Education Services: Courses offered over commercial television, appearances on a series of programs over television and radio for public relations and information (about 200 a year), closed-circuit television for teacher train-

ing, television film and radio facilities for professional instruction, film projectors, slide projectors, opaque projectors, overhead projectors, our own course materials reproduced on Xerox, mimeo., etc., as well as traditional aids.

2. Roanoke College: Closed-circuit TV, educational TV, movies, drama, string overhead usage; models, slides; maps, globes, etc.

VII. Student Recruitment

I. Publicity

	Much	Limited	Very Little	None
A. Newspaper	85	1	-	2
B. Radio	30	4	1	20
C. Television	20	4	3	25

II. Public Relations - Special Motivational Appeals Developed For

A. Industry	30	6	6
	Yes	No	Limited

B. Organizations

1. Chambers of Commerce	10	25	5
	Yes	No	Limited

2. Clubs (Kiwanis, Rotarians, etc.)	12	50	3
	Yes	No	Limited

The University of Akron, Akron, Ohio
Evening College

Total enrollment 14,500   Public Institution
Evening enrollment 5,300,   Quarter System
  non-credit 1,700+

I. Admission Policies

Deadline for application for admission to evening classes is as late as open registration which is about two weeks prior to registration. Students who register without transcripts are classified as "pending" until transcripts are received. Non-matriculated students may take a maximum of 15 quarter hours. Admission requirements for special students are recommendation of his Dean that experience qualifies him to take certain courses; regular students must be

The University of Akron (cont.)

high school graduates; submit ACT or CEEB scores; or be
in good academic standing at the last college attended. Mail
registration is used. Students must maintain a 2.0 GPA to
remain in good standing. There is no special degree program for adults. Admission Policies are set by the Undergraduate Admissions Committee of the University Council--
the Evening College Dean is a member. There is an orientation for evening students.

II. Terminology

Title of Division: Evening College, defined: The
Evening College administers the operation of the academic
programs of the several degree granting colleges within the
University which occur after 5 p. m. The term "College" implies that it is possible to obtain a degree by going evenings
only. Continuing Education is a life-long process of study
by adults utilizing periodic learning experiences supported by
the University resources and within a University environment
featuring program and patterns designed (not adapted) for
adults and taught by faculty familiar with adult student needs.

III. Fees

There is no fee differential between day and evening
classes.

IV. Faculty and Faculty Recruitment

80% teaching evening classes are full time. Final
authority to hire full-time faculty members lies with the
Dean of the College in which he will teach; part-time evening faculty are hired by the Dean of the Evening College after academic screening by the Dean of the College in which
the course he will teach is offered. The Dean of the Evening College may reject a faculty member assigned to teach
evening classes. Faculty meetings are held once every
quarter with part-time faculty members teaching evening
classes. Faculty members are permitted to teach overloads
if it is done with the knowledge and consent of the Dean involved.

V. Scheduling

The Dean of the Evening College is responsible for
the evening class schedule and has the authority to revise it.
Three credit hour courses are scheduled two nights a week.
Day and evening classes are equal in terms of quality. Evening students are eligible for the dean's list only if they
carry 12 quarter hours per term with a GPA of 3. 25 or better, most evening students do not take that many courses.

VI. General

Tutorial projects are staffed by volunteer students and
faculty in 10 ghetto areas and are sponsored by OEO. Several students participate in discussions regarding academic program through standing committees of the University Council.
The evening division is receiving adequate support. The
Dean of the Evening College is responsible to the Vice-President for Academic Affairs. Audio-visual instructional aids
are available for evening classes.

VII. Student Recruitment

Newspaper and radio publicity are used. Special motivational appeals have been developed for Industry and Civic
Organizations.

* * *

American International College, Springfield, Mass.
Evening College
Total enrollment 1, 760 day   Private Institution
Evening enrollment 1, 075 eve-   Semester System
   ning; off-campus 500

I. Admissions Policies

Deadline for application for evening classes is the day
classes start. Students may register for credit courses
without transcripts. Non-matriculated students may take a
maximum of 18 semester hours. Admission requirements
are high school graduation and in some cases specific course
requirements. Mail registration is used. There is an annual review of each student's records and an interview with
each student whose record is unsatisfactory. There is no

American International College (cont.)

special degree for adults. Admission policies are set by the day school faculty. Day and evening students may register in the same classes with permission. Orientation for evening students is held a week before classes start.

II. Terminology

Title of Division: Evening College, defined: College which offers only on-campus evening credit courses.

III. Fees

Tuition fees are the same for day, evening, graduate and undergraduate courses. Refunds are made on a graduated percentage basis.

IV. Faculty and Faculty Recruitment

62% teaching evening classes are full time. Final authority to hire faculty lies with day school department chairmen, although some hiring is done by the Dean of the Evening College. The Dean of the Evening College can engage an instructor without the consent of the department chairmen. No regular faculty meetings are held. Faculty members are limited to one overload course per semester; conferences, etc., do not count.

V. Scheduling

The Dean of the Evening College is responsible for the evening class schedule, and has the authority to revise it. Three credit hour courses are scheduled one night a week. Day and evening classes are equal in terms of quality. There is no Dean's List for evening students, there is an honor society: Alpha Sigma Lambda.

VI. General

Special courses for economically deprived populations are being planned. Students participate in discussions regarding academic programs through the Evening Student Council and through voting memberships on the Committee for Eve-

ning and Summer Curricula. The evening division is receiving adequate support. The Dean of the Evening College
is responsible to the President of the College. Audio-visual
instructional aids are available for use in evening classes.

VII. Student Recruitment

Newspaper, radio and television publicity are used.
Special motivational appeals have been developed for industry.

* * *

The American University
Washington, D. C.
College of Continuing Education

Total enrollment: Church-related Institution
  4, 800 off-campus   Semester System
  4, 200 on-campus

I. Admission Policies

There is no deadline for application for admission for
non-degree or special students; regular students must apply
about four months prior to registration, if they are transfer-
ring from another college, two months prior. Non-degree
may take a maximum of 30 hours. Admission requirements
are at least 21 years of age and in good standing at college
previously attended. Mail registration will be used in the
future. Non-degree students are required to maintain a "C"
average. ACT or CEEB tests are required only of students
applying for degree status. Degree Programs for adults are
as follows: Bachelor of Science in General Studies, Master
of Science in Teaching, B. S. in Law Enforcement and MS in
Correctional Administration. Admission requirements are
the same as other degree programs. Admission policies are
set by the Admissions Committee. Day and evening students
may enroll in the same classes. There is no special orientation for evening students; it is included with the regular day
program.

II. Terminology

Title of Division: College of Continuing Education,
defined: A college designed to act as a link between the
adult student and the University. CCE enables the adult student to make maximum use of University facilities. Con-

65

The American University (cont.)

tinuing Education defined: The provision of a means for the continuing pursuit of learning--via non-degree, degree and non-credit programs.

III. Fees

There is a fee differential between on and off-campus courses because there is a lower overhead off-campus. Refunds are made on a graduated scale from the first six (6) weeks of classes.

IV. Faculty and Faculty Recruitment

There is no policy regarding the percentage of faculty for evening classes that are full-time faculty members. Final authority to hire evening faculty lies with the Dean of the College of Continuing Education. Recommendations regarding faculty are usually followed by Department Chairmen. No full-time faculty members teach exclusively in the evening. No regular faculty meetings are held.

V. Scheduling

The Dean of the College of Continuing Education is responsible only for the off-campus class schedule. The Dean of CCE has the authority to revise the schedule. Three credit courses are scheduled one night a week. Various research projects through the Labor Studies Center have been done under the TITLE I Project. Part-time evening students are not eligible for the Dean's List.

VI. General

In general, all evening divisions are not receiving adequate support. The Dean of the College of Continuing Education is responsible to the Provost. Audio-visual instructional aids are available for evening classes.

VII. Student Recruitment

Newspaper, radio and television publicity are used.

Special motivational appeals have been developed for Industry and Organizations and is handled through the University Public Relations Department.

* * *

Babson Institute, Babson Park, Mass.
Continuing Education Division

Total enrollment 834	Private Institution
Evening enrollment 430	Trimester System evenings; Terms, days

I. Admission Policies

Deadline for application for admission to evening classes is prior to start of classes. Students may register for credit courses in some cases without transcripts. Students in the graduate school may take credit courses without matriculating. Mail registration is used. The special degree for adults: Master of Business Administration, with an enrollment of 430. Requirements for degree program are B. A. or B. S. with a 2. 8 on a 4. 0 basis. Admission policies are set by the faculty; and for non-matriculating or special students, the Dean of Continuing Education. Day and evening students enroll in the same classes on a very limited basis. There is no orientation for evening students.

II. Terminology

Title of Division: Continuing Education Division.

III. Fees

Day school tuition is $1, 800; $150 per course; evening fees are $125 per course. Refunds are made on a graduated percentage basis.

IV. Faculty and Faculty Recruitment

33% teaching evening classes are full-time. Final authority to hire faculty lies with the Dean of Faculty. No regular faculty meetings are held. Overloads are not permitted on a credit basis to insure that faculty members do a good job for what they teach regularly.

Babson Institute (cont.)

V. Scheduling

The Registrar is responsible for the evening class schedule. Two 2/3 credit hour courses are scheduled for two successive 65 minute sessions in one night for 16 weeks. There is no Dean's List for part-time evening students.

VI. General

The evening division is receiving adequate support. The Dean of Continuing Education is responsible to the President. Most audio-visual instructional aids are available but more are needed.

VII. Student Recruitment

Newspaper and radio publicity are used. Special motivational appeals have been developed for industry and civic organizations.

* * *

Bloomfield College
Evening College

Total enrollment 1,100   Private, Church-related
Evening enrollment 675   Institution
     Semester System

I. Admission Policies

There is no deadline for application for admission. A maximum of 18 hours may be taken by non-matriculating students. Admission requirements are high school graduation and interest in field of study. Students must maintain 1.6 in freshman year; 1.8 in sophomore year; 2.0 in junior and senior years. There is no special degree program for adults. Admission policies are set by the Administrative Committee, composed of faculty members, as well as the Director of the Evening Division. Orientation for evening students is on the first night of classes each semester.

68

II. Terminology

Title of Division: Evening College, defined, adjunct of day college.

III. Fees

Evening students pay $40 per credit hour up to 12 hours and then are required to pay the same tuition as day students. Refunds are 80% first week of classes; 60% second week, 40% third week and 20% fourth week.

IV. Faculty and Faculty Recruitment

Approximately 90% teaching evening classes are full-time. Final authority to hire evening faculty lies with the dean of the college. No regular faculty meetings are held. Faculty members teaching an overload are paid an additional stipend; however, this practice is not encouraged.

V. Scheduling

The Director of the Evening Session is responsible for the evening class schedule. Three credit hour classes are held two nights per week. Part-time evening students are eligible for the dean's list with 3. 2 after completing six credit hours.

VI. General

Evening Division is receiving adequate support. The Director of the evening and summer session is responsible to the dean of the college.

VII. Student Recruitment

Newspaper publicity is used. Special motivational appeals have been made to industry, and organizations such as the Chamber of Commerce, clubs, etc.

* * *

Boston College
Evening College

Total enrollment 9,972   Private, Church-related
Evening enrollment 918   Institution

I. Admission Policies

No deadline for application for admission, but entrance
exam is required. Students may register without transcripts
as "special students." There is no limit to amount of hours
taken as a non-matriculating special student. Admission requirements are high school graduation or equivalent. Tests
required for degree students: SCAT and Cooperative Eng-
lish/Reading Test. There is no mail registration. Student
is required to maintain a "C-" average or be placed on probation. At least a "C-" average required for graduation. No
special degree program for adults is offered. Admission
policies are set by Academic Council of Evening College.
A few day students enroll in evening classes. There is an
orientation program for evening students.

II. Terminology

Title of Division: Evening College of Arts and Sciences and Business; defined: The undergraduate division of
the university offering evening degree programs and credit
courses for the part-time student.

III. Fees

Day tuition is $200 per course; evening tuition is $135
per 3-credit course. Tuition for any course is proportionally refundable; after fifth week of class no refund.

IV. Faculty and Faculty Recruitment

90% teaching evening classes are full-time faculty
members. Authority to hire faculty lies with Department
Chairmen and College Deans. No full-time faculty teach only
in the evening. Most regular faculty teach in evening as an
overload.

70

V. Scheduling

Dean responsible for schedule. One night three credit hour courses are preferable. Quality of day and evening
classes are equal. Part-time students are eligible for the
Dean's List with 82% average or better in any semester in
which they complete nine credit hours.

VI. General

Evening College is receiving adequate support. Dean
is responsible to Academic Vice-President. Newspaper publicity is used.

* * *

Boston University, Boston, Mass.
Metropolitan College

Total enrollment 22, 960   Private Institution
Evening enrollment 3, 000   Semester System

I. Admission Policies

There is a deadline for application for admission to
evening classes. Students may register for credit courses
without transcripts providing they meet the course prerequisites. Non-matriculated students may accumulate an unlimited amount of credit courses. Admission requirements for
special students is high school diploma; regular students,
high school grades, SAT, and performance. Mail registration is used. Students must maintain a 2. 0 for graduation.
The Master of Liberal Arts is offered as a special degree
for adults; 19 students are enrolled in this degree program.
Admission is competitive with a "B" average or better in latter half of undergraduate program the basic criterion. Admission policies are set by the Faculty Board of the College.
Day and evening students may enroll in the same classes.
Evening students meet faculty and staff at the general open-
house during registration.

II. Terminology

Title of Division: Metropolitan College, defined: Evening College which offers part-time degree programs and degree credit for matriculated and non-matriculated students.

71

Boston University (cont.)

III. Fees

Day tuition is $58 per credit hour; evening tuition is $40 per credit hour. Refunds are made on a graduating percentage basis.

IV. Faculty and Faculty Recruitment

35% teaching evening classes are full-time University faculty. Final authority to hire faculty lies with the Dean of the Metropolitan College. The Dean can reject a faculty member assigned to teach evening classes and may engage an instructor without the consent of the department head if he refuses to staff evening classes. Overloads of one course per semester are permitted for each faculty member.

V. Scheduling

The Registrar, Dean and Department Chairmen are responsible for the evening class schedule. The Dean has the authority to revise the evening class schedule. Three credit hour courses are scheduled both one and two nights per week. There is no Dean's List.

VI. General

There are special and new credit degrees in Urban Affairs (undergraduate and graduate) and Master Liberal Studies. The Evening Division is receiving adequate support. The Dean of the Metropolitan College is responsible to the Vice President of Academic Affairs. Audio-visual instructional aids are available for evening classes.

VII. Student Recruitment

Newspaper and radio publicity are used. Special motivational appeals have been developed for community organizations.

* * *

University of Bridgeport
Evening Division

Total enrollment 8,500   Private Institution
Evening Division 4,300   Semester System

I. Admission Policies

Deadline for admission, two months prior to registration. Students may register for credit without transcripts. 15-30 semester hours limit for non-matriculating students. Admission requirement is high school graduation. No mail registration is used. Dismissal for all students with 15 quality points deficiency. No ACT or CEEB tests required. No special degree program and not considered. Admission policies are set by Academic Standards Committee of regular faculty. Mixed classes--day and evening students are allowed to register for same class if space is available because it allows more flexibility for evening students.

II. Terminology

Title of Division: Evening Division, defined: A Division of the University primarily concerned with a series of credit and non-credit courses, conferences and institutes and, in addition, it actually encompasses all phases of part-time study done by adults.

III. Fees

Evening students pay tuition only. Only eligible for counseling services. Refunds based on full tution--after one week, 90%; two weeks, 80%; three weeks, 50%; longer, no refund.

IV. Faculty and Faculty Recruitment

85% teaching evening classes are full-time. Final authority to hire evening faculty lies with Department Chairmen. The evening faculty members are responsible to the Department Chairmen. Faculty meetings are held on Friday and Sunday afternoons.

University of Bridgeport (cont.)

V. Scheduling

The Director of the Evening Division is responsible for the schedule. Departments send suggestions concerning problems with schedules directly to the registrar. Three credit hour classes are held two nights a week. There is no difference in the quality of day and evening classes. Part-time students are not eligible for the Dean's List. We do have a chapter of Alpha Sigma Lambda.

VI. General

Evening Division is receiving adequate support. As Director of the Evening Division, he is responsible to the new Vice-President for Academic Affairs. Audio-visual aids, e.g., T.V., projectors, etc.

VII. Student Recruitment

Newspaper and Radio Publicity are used. Public Relations-Special motivational appeals have been developed for Industry and Organizations (Chamber of Commerce, Kiwanis, Rotarians).

* * *

Brigham Young University
Department of Evening Classes
in Division of Continuing Education

Total enrollment 22,300   Private, church-related
Evening enrollment 6,523   Institution
Semester System

I. Admission Policies

Applications for admission to evening classes are accepted through the first week and a half of classes. Regular students are required to apply approximately two weeks prior to registration. Students taking evening classes, only, may register without transcripts. A full load may be taken by non-matriculating students. Admission requirements for non-matriculating students are high school graduation or 19 years of age. Mail registration is used. Counselors maintain a "history" card on students and use it to guide them in advising. A special degree program for adults is being considered. Admission policies are set by the administrators in the Department of Evening Classes, the Dean of Continuing Education, and the Administrative Council of the University. Day and evening students may enroll in the same classes. Orientation for evening students is included with the day school program.

II. Terminology

Title of Division: Department of Evening Classes in the Division of Continuing Education, defined: campus credit classes for evening students.

III. Fees

The fees are exactly the same for day and evening classes. If a student withdraws after the beginning of the class, he forfeits twelve and one half percent of his fees for each one sixteenth of the class offered to date. No refunds are made after the middle of the courses; full refunds are made for cancelled classes.

IV. Faculty and Faculty Recruitment

95% teaching evening classes are taken from day faculty. The final authority to hire faculty lies with the Dean of the Division of Continuing Education and Chairman of the Department of Evening Classes. The Chairman of Evening Classes can reject a faculty member assigned to teach evening classes. An overload of six hours of credit per academic year is permitted, including evening.

V. Scheduling

The Chairman is responsible for the evening class schedule, and has the authority to make changes in it. Three credit hour classes are scheduled one night a week, four and five hour courses, two nights a week. Part-time evening students are eligible for the Dean's List. Magna cum laude is awarded to students with 45 hours of 3.80 or higher, cum laude with 45 hours of 3.5 to 3.79.

Brigham Young University (cont.)

VI. General

Students participate in discussions regarding the academic program with counselors and administrators and one student is a member of the Evening Classes Advisory Council. The evening division is receiving adequate support. The Chairman of Evening Classes is responsible to the Dean of Continuing Education. All audio-visual instructional materials are available.

VII. Student Recruitment

Newspaper (seven local newspapers), radio and television publicity are used. Special motivational appeals have been developed for industry and organizations in cooperation with other institutions and technical colleges.

* * *

University of British Columbia
Vancouver, B. C.

Extra-Sessional Credit
Total enrollment 17,800 (1967-68)
Evening enrollment 1,825

I. Admission Policies

Deadline for application for admission to evening classes for returning students is six weeks and sooner for students entering for the first time. Students may not register for credit courses before transcripts are received. Non-matriculated students may take credit work but credit is not given until students matriculate. Non-matriculating students must be at least 23 years old; regular students must meet the requirements for regular day students. Mail registration is used. A special degree for adults is being considered. Admission policies are set by the University Senate.

II. Terminology

Title of Division: Extra-Sessional Credit, defined: Regular university courses for the student pursuing his degree by part-time, scheduled at times most convenient for this student.

76

III. Fees

There is no fee differential between day and evening classes for credit courses.

IV. Faculty and Faculty Recruitment

90% teaching evening classes are full-time. Final authority to hire faculty lies with Department Chairmen. No regular faculty meetings are held. Faculty members who participate in institutes, conferences, etc., do so on an overload basis.

V. Scheduling

The Director of Extra-Sessional Credit is responsible for the evening class schedule, and has the authority to revise it. Three credit hour courses are scheduled both one and two nights a week. Day and evening classes are equal in terms of quality.

VI. General

In general, evening division are not receiving adequate support. The Administrator of the Extra-Sessional Credit is responsible to the Director of the Extension Department. Audio-visual instructional aids are available for use in evening classes.

VII. Student Recruitment

Newspaper publicity is used but a special brochure is used also. Special appeals have been developed for Teachers' Organizations.

* * *

Bronx Community College
Bronx, N. Y.

Evening and Continuing Education
Total enrollment 7, 500   Public Institution
Evening enrollment 4, 500

Bronx Community College (cont.)

I. Admission Policies

There is no deadline for application for admission to evening classes. Students may register for credit courses without transcripts. Non-matriculated students are limited to 6 credits for two courses depending on preparation. Regular students are selected by use of cut-off scores based on high school average and CEEB scores after eligibility through high school unit requirements for the particular curriculum. Mail registration is used. There is no special degree for adults. Admission policies are set by CUNY. Day and evening students may register in the same classes. There is an orientation for evening students once a week for the first three weeks of classes.

II. Terminology

Title of Division: Evening and Continuing Education, defined: All courses and programs other than those designed to meet the needs of the matriculated student attending in the day.

III. Fees

Matriculating students go tuition free; non-matriculants pay fees for courses.

IV. Faculty and Faculty Recruitment

15% teaching evening classes are full-time. Final authority to hire faculty lies with the Dean of Evening and Continuing Education. Full-time faculty members who teach exclusively in the evening are responsible to the Dean through the Department Chairmen. No regular faculty meetings are held. Overloads are limited to a maximum of 8 course hours per year.

V. Scheduling

The Dean of Evening and Continuing Education is responsible for the evening class schedule, and has the authority to revise it. Three credit hour classes are scheduled two nights a week. Day and evening classes are equal in terms of quality. Part-time evening students are eligible for the Dean's List.

VI. General

Students participate some in discussions regarding the academic program. In general, all evening divisions are not receiving adequate support. The Dean of the Evening Continuing Education is responsible to the President. Audiovisual instructional aids are available for use in evening classes.

VII. Student Recruitment

Newspaper publicity is used.

* * *

Brooklyn College of the City University of New York
School of General Studies
Total enrollment 30,000   Public Institution
Evening enrollment 9,000   Semester System

I. Admission Policies

Application for admission to evening classes must be made approximately one month before registration. Students may not register for credit courses without transcripts. There is no limit to the amount of courses taken as a non-matriculating student. Admission requirements for adult students are satisfactory high school or college records and evidence of adequate preparation for specific courses. Qualifying examinations are required of adults in the evening division. A special degree program for adults is offered: Special Baccalaureate Degree Program for Adults (enrollment: 150). Admission policies are set by the Director of Admissions and a committee on Admission Requirements. Day and evening students may enroll in the same classes with approval. Orientation programs are held each semester for evening students.

Brooklyn College of the City Univ. of N. Y. (cont.)

II. Terminology

Title of Division: School of General Studies, defined: "Its primary objective is to offer higher educational opportunities to working men and women."

III. Fees

Proportional refunds are made to students within the first three weeks of the term.

IV. Faculty and Faculty Recruitment

There are approximately 60 full-time and 500 part-time faculty members. Final authority for hiring faculty lies with the teaching departments and the Dean of the School of General Studies with approval by the Board of Higher Education. The Dean of the School of General Studies can reject a faculty member assigned to teach evening classes. Sixty full-time faculty members teach exclusively in the evening and are responsible to their respective departments. Regular faculty meetings are held once or twice yearly. Faculty members are allowed to teach an overload of 8 semester hours per year.

V. Scheduling

The Dean of the School of General Studies is responsible for the schedule of evening classes. Departments submit tentative schedules to Dean and they are revised where necessary. Three credit hour classes are scheduled twice weekly. Part-time students are eligible for the Dean's List with a 3.3 grade point average after completing 30 credit hours.

VI. General

Some credit and non-credit courses are offered off-campus for economically deprived populations. Students participate in discussion regarding academic programs by serving on faculty-student committees. In general, evening divisions are not receiving adequate support. The Dean of the School of General Studies is responsible to the President. Complete audio-visual instructional aids are available for evening classes.

VII. Student Recruitment

Newspaper and radio publicity are used. Special motivational appeals have been developed for industry and organizations.

* * *

Bryant College
Providence, Rhode Island

Evening Division
Total enrollment 1, 950   Private Institution
Evening enrollment 1, 430   Semester System

I. Admission Policies

Deadline for application for admission to evening classes is about two weeks prior to registration. Students may register for credit courses without transcripts and may take a maximum of 12 credit hours as non-matriculating students. Admission requirements for students are high school graduation or equivalency; in law enforcement classes, students must be in some phase of law enforcement work; insurance classes, in insurance work, etc. Mail registration will be used in January 1969. Students must maintain a 2.0 quality point average for graduation; if average falls below 1.6, students are counseled. A special degree program is not offered, but there are special certificate programs for adults in various fields. Admission policies are set by the Vice-President of Academic Affairs and the Dean and Director of the Evening Division. Day and evening students may register in the same classes with Dean's permission. There is no orientation program for evening students.

II. Terminology

Title of Division: Evening Division of Bryant College, defined: Division responsible for adult education, degrees and (non-credit) special courses, evening and Saturdays, on and off campus. Continuing Education, defined: Services to

Bryant College (cont.)

help a person who needs more knowledge during his lifetime
than he can obtain in normal high school and college. With
rapidly advancing technology in all fields, continuing education is of greater importance than any other previous period
in history.

III. Fees

Day students pay $45 per semester hour; evening stu-
dents pay $16. 67 per semester hour. Refunds are made on
a graduating percentage basis: 80% first week; 60% second
week; 40% third week; after, no refund.

IV. Faculty and Faculty Recruitment

50% teaching evening classes are full-time faculty
members. Final authority to hire evening part-time faculty
lies with the Director and Dean of the Evening Division. No
full-time faculty members teach exclusively in the evening.
The Dean can hire part-time instructors. Regular faculty
meetings are held the week before each semester begins.
Full-time faculty members are limited to teaching not more
than two nights a week (six semester hours) in the evening
division.

V. Scheduling

The Dean of the Evening Division is responsible for
the evening class schedule and has the authority to revise
it. Three credit hour classes are scheduled both one and
two nights a week. Day and evening classes are equal in
terms of quality. There is no Dean's List.

VI. General

Some special courses for economically deprived populations are planned. Day students participate in discussions
regarding the academic program more than evening students.
Special off-campus and Saturday classes are offered for Law
Enforcement Personnel.

* * *

Carnegie-Mellon University
Evening Classes and Summer Sessions
Pittsburgh, Pennsylvania
Total enrollment 4, 200   Private Institution
Evening enrollment 1, 200
plus 600-700 day students

I. Admission Policies

Deadline for application for admission to evening
classes is the day of registration. Students may not register
for credit courses without transcripts. Non-matriculated or
"special" students may take an unlimited amount of credit
work. Admission requirements are upper one-third of high
school graduating class and CEEB scores. Mail is used for
registration forms and payment of fees. Students must maintain a "C" average. CEEB scores are required for adults in
the evening. There is no special degree for adults. Admission policies are set by the Day Admissions Committee.
Day students may register for evening classes in order to
avoid conflicts in scheduling. There is no orientation for
evening students, instead, individual conferences.

II. Terminology

Title of Division: Evening Classes and Summer Sessions, defined: An extension of the regular day program.

III. Fees

Evening charges per credit are approximately the
same as the day which is based on a flat rate. Refunds are
made up to the fifth week of classes.

IV. Faculty and Faculty Recruitment

45% teaching evening classes are full-time faculty
members. Full-time faculty members are hired by departments; part-time members with approval of the Evening Director. No full-time faculty teach exclusively in the evening.
Regular faculty meetings are not held. No overloads are
permitted; assignments are part of regular loads.

83

Carnegie-Mellon University (cont.)

V. Scheduling

The registrar is responsible for all schedules. The Evening Director has the authority to revise the schedule. Three credit-hour courses are scheduled both one and two nights a week. Day and evening classes are equal in terms of quality. Part-time evening students are not eligible for the Dean's List.

VI. General

Day students participate in discussions regarding the academic program; evening students do not. In general, all evening divisions are not receiving adequate support. The Director of Evening Classes is responsible to the Vice-President for Academic Affairs. Audio-visual instructional aids are available for use in evening classes.

VII. Student Recruitment

Newspaper publicity is used. Special motivational appeals have been developed for industry.

* * *

Centenary College of Louisiana
Evening Division

Total enrollment 1,150   Private, Church-related
Evening enrollment 297   Institution
                                  Semester System

I. Admission Policies

Deadline for application is date of registration. Students may enroll for credit without transcripts provided they sign an "eligibility statement." All students must matriculate as degree students. Admission requirement is high school graduation with 2.0 average or GED. Mail registration is not a practice. Students must attend classes regularly and maintain a "C" average. ACT and CEEB not required. No special degree program offered and not considered. Admission policies are set by the Admissions Office in consultation with the Dean of the Evening Division. Day and evening students may enroll in the same classes. There is no orientation for evening students.

II. Terminology

Title of Division: Evening Division: a part of the College. Continuing Education, defined: "Non-degree, evening courses offered for adults, senior citizens and the like."

III. Fees

Evening students pay $35 a semester hour, day students $40 a semester hour, justification: Evening Division faculty are paid lower salaries. Application fee is not refundable. If a student withdraws completely within one month of graduation, he receives 50% of his tuition. There is no refund for partial withdrawals.

IV. Faculty and Faculty Recruitment

33% teaching evening classes are full-time. Final authority to hire a faculty member lies with the Director of the Evening Division. The Director can reject a faculty member assigned to teach evening classes. Regular faculty meetings are held the beginning and end of each semester.

V. Scheduling

The Director is responsible for the schedule. The procedure: Schedule is worked out in consultation with the department chairmen, based on needs of students and acceptance of courses by students. Day and evening classes are equal in terms of quality. Part-time students are not eligible for the Dean's List.

VI. General

Two students or more are on all policy-making committees of the university. Evening Division, in general, are not receiving adequate support. The director is responsible to the Academic Dean. Audio-visual equipment is available for use in instruction.

Centenary College of Louisiana (cont.)

VII.   Student Recruitment

Newspaper publicity (3 times a year) and radio announcements are used.   Appeals are now being made to industry and have been made in the past to the Chamber of Commerce.

* * *

University of Chattanooga
Chattanooga College

Total enrollment 2,600	Private (State after July
Evening enrollment 1,100 (in-	1, 1969)
cludes day students enrolled	Semester System
in evening classes)	

I.   Admission Policies

Deadline for application for admission is two weeks prior to registration.   Students may register for regular credit courses without transcripts only with approval by the Director of Admissions.   Students desiring regular college credit must meet the same standards for admission as those entering day classes.   As an entrance examination, evening students may take SCAT in lieu of ACT or CEEB.   Students who have attained the age of 21 and have sufficient educational background and experience to profit from courses desired may register as Adult Specials for non-degree credit without meeting regular admission standards.   Students must maintain at least the following grade point average: 1.50 after 24 hours; 1.75 after 60 hours; 1.85 after 90 hours.   Students on probation must maintain a 2.0 average.   There is no special degree program for adults but one is being considered. Admission policies are set by the Admission Committee and Faculty Council.

II.   Terminology

Title of Division: Chattanooga College defined: The evening and special classes division of the University.

III.   Fees

Tuition: part-time day students, $40 per semester

hour; part-time evening students, $30 per semester hour; day students have some services not available to evening students.

IV. Faculty and Faculty Recruitment

50% teaching evening classes are full-time faculty members and this is considered satisfactory. Final authority to hire part-time evening faculty lies with the Dean of the Evening Division. Overloads for regular faculty members are not permitted in credit courses, but limited participation in seminars without additional compensation is approved.

V. Scheduling

The Dean is responsible for the evening class schedule: it is compiled in the Dean's Office. Three credit hour classes are scheduled two nights a week. A self-study project was undertaken by the Chattanooga College Committee in 1967. Part-time students are not eligible for the Dean's List.

VI. General

Students participate in discussions regarding the academic program through conferences with deans and counselors and express opinions through questionnaires. The evening division lacks adequate support in some area of operation. The Dean of Chattanooga College is responsible to the President of the University. Complete audio-visual instructional aids are available for evening classes.

VII. Student Recruitment

Newspaper articles and advertisements as well as radio and television publicity are used. Special motivational appeals have been developed for business and industry in the form of brochures for special programs for employees. The Chamber of Commerce, The Society for the Advancement of Management and other organizations in the area assist in promoting community service programs.

* * *

University of Cincinnati
Evening College

Total enrollment 31, 000   Public (City and State
Evening enrollment 11, 245 credit,   Institution
3, 000 non-credit   Quarter System

I. Admission Policies

Deadline for application for admission is approximately two days prior to registration. Students may register provisionally without transcripts. Students may take courses approved by advisors without being classified as degree candidates. Admission requirement is graduation from an accredited high school or equivalent. Mail registration is used; 45% of the student body took advantage of mail registration in Fall Quarter. A special degree for adults is offered: Bachelor of Science: (Enrollment 3, 000+). All students following undergraduate or graduate degree programs are required to matriculate. Admission requirements are basically set by the Board of Regents. Day and evening students may enroll in the same class.

II. Terminology

Title of Division: Evening College, defined: a college that offers its own associate and bachelor degrees; offers graduate work in cooperation with Graduate School; controls its own faculty and has identical status as other campus colleges. Refund policies: week prior to first week of quarter--100%; first and second week--80%; third week--60%; fourth week--40%; fifth week--20%; after fifth week--no refund allowed.

III. Fees

Undergraduate: Quarter Credit Hour, Cincinnati-- $11., Other Ohio--$16., Out of State--$27. Graduate: Quarter Credit Hour, Cincinnati--$16., Other Ohio--$25., Out of State--$35.

IV. Faculty and Faculty Recruitment

Two-thirds of the faculty are full-time and one-third part-time off-campus members. No full-time faculty teach

88

exclusively for the Evening College. Final authority to hire faculty lies with the Evening College Dean. Regular faculty meetings are held as needed at a minimum of once a year. Faculty members are permitted to teach two hours as an overload and in some cases up to four depending on individual situations.

V. Scheduling

The Dean of the Evening College is responsible for the schedule of evening classes. Most three credit hour classes are scheduled one night a week and some two nights. Part-time students are eligible for the Dean's List on completing six quarter hours with a minimum of 3.5 average. A Dean's List is published at the end of each quarter.

VI. General

Some non-credit courses are planned in off-campus locations for economically deprived populations. Some evening activities are not receiving adequate support. The Dean of the Evening College is responsible to the Provost for Academic Affairs. Audio-visual aids are available for Evening Classes.

VII. Student Recruitment

Newspaper, radio, and television publicity are used. Special motivational appeals have been developed for industry and organizations including civic and professional groups.

* * *

The Citadel
Evening Program
Total enrollment 2,350   Public (State) Institution
Evening enrollment 300   Semester System

I. Admission Policies

Deadline for application for admission is one week before classes begin. A student may not register for credit until transcripts are received. There is no limit to the amount of credit work taken as a non-degree student. Admission requirements are high school graduation or good stand-

The Citadel (cont.)

ing in previous college.   Mail registration is used.   ACT and
CEEB exams are not required.   A special two-year associate degree is offered by the name: Associate in Liberal Arts
or Business Administration.   Admission requirements for
this program are the same as regular requirements.   Admission policies are set by a Faculty Evening Program Committee with approval of Academic Dean.   Day and Evening
do not enroll in the same class.

II.   Terminology

The Citadel Evening Program, defined: "College
courses for those desiring a continuation of a college education, or for advancement in employment or a general broad-
ening of interests."

III.   Fees

Cost for day students include student fees and appro-
priations made by the state of South Carolina.   Evening program fees include registration fee and $20 per semester
hour.   Justification: Evening Program has no state supported funds.   Refunds to students are not made after the
second week of class.

IV.   Faculty and Faculty Recruitment

All evening faculty are full-time day faculty.   The authority to hire faculty lies with department chairmen.   No
regular faculty meetings.   Faculty are permitted one overload class.

V.   Scheduling

The Director is responsible for scheduling.   Both one
night and two nights are used to schedule three credit hour
classes.   In some respects, the evening classes have more
mature students with better results, academically.   Part-
time students are not eligible for the Dean's List.

VI. General

In general, evening divisions are not receiving adequate support. The Director of the Evening Program is responsible to the Vice-President of the College. Audio-visual aids are available.

VII. Student Recruitment

Newspaper articles and advertisements are used for publicity, as well as radio and television announcements. Public relations: Special courses designed for particular interest to industry have been organized.

* * *

City College of New York
School of General Studies
New York, New York
Total enrollment 15,00 approx.   Public Institution
Evening enrollment 4,200

I. Admission Policies

There is a deadline for application for admission to evening classes but exceptions are made.   Students may not register for credit courses without transcripts.   Non-matriculated students may take an unlimited amount of work but they must take courses required for a degree.   Admission requirements are high school graduation and SCAT scores. Mail registration is not used.   Students must maintain a "C" average.   There is no special degree for adults.   Admission policies are set by the college as a whole for regular students and by the School of General Studies in consultation with the General Admissions Office.   Day and evening students may enroll in the same classes.   There is an orientation program for evening students.

II. Terminology

Title of Division: School of General Studies, defined: Evening Session for same baccalaureate degrees as those offered in day.   Continuing Education: All education, both formal and informal, continues some previous education.

III. Fees

Matriculated students pay no tuition; non-matriculated students pay $18 per class hour. City government has felt that only those who met rigid entrance requirements were to be given free tuition. Refunds are made on a graduating percentage basis unless the student is entering the armed forces.

IV. Faculty and Faculty Recruitment

50% teaching evening classes are full-time faculty members: the same percentage students who are matriculated. Final authority to hire faculty lies with the departments. The Dean can reject a faculty member assigned to teach evening classes. Some full-time faculty members teach exclusively in the evening. They are responsible to their department chairmen. Regular faculty meetings are not held. A maximum of 8 class hours are permitted for overloads per year.

V. Scheduling

The Dean of the School of General Studies is responsible for the evening class schedule. The Dean has the authority to revise the evening class schedule in consultation with the departments. Three credit hour courses are scheduled two nights a wekk. Part-time evening students are eligible for the Dean's List with at least 32 hours with a 3. 2 (A=4). Motivation seems to be a very important factor in determining success. High School average and "aptitude" tests do not predict well enough.

VI. General

Students participate in discussions regarding the academic program by meeting regularly with the Committee on Curriculum. In general, all evening divisions are not receiving adequate support. The Dean of the School of General Studies is responsible to the President of the College.

* * *

Cleveland College of Case Western Reserve University
Cleveland, Ohio
University Continuing Education Division
Total enrollment 1,004   Private Institution
Semester System

I. Admission Policies

Deadline for application for admission to evening classes is the first day of class. Non-degree students may register for credit courses without transcripts. Non-matriculated students may take a maximum of 45 hours. Admission requirements for non-degree students are at least 21 years of age, high school graduation and a Cleveland College counselor's assessment of ability to do college work. Recent college attendance necessitates application for admission to the degree program. Students with degrees are allowed to take undergraduate courses only. Mail registration is used. After completing 30 hours students must maintain a prescribed grade point average. There is no special degree program for adults. Admission policies are set by the University Admissions Office for regular degree students; for non-matriculated or "special" students, requirements are set by the Dean's Office and counseling section of Cleveland College. Day and evening students may enroll in the same classes. There is no orientation for evening students.

II. Terminology

Title of Division: University Continuing Education Division, defined: A program which allows the intellectually qualified high school graduate of any age to enroll in part or full-time study which may or may not lead to a degree.

III. Fees

There is no fee differential between day and evening classes. Refunds are made on a graduating percentage basis.

IV. Faculty and Faculty Recruitment

There is no policy regarding the percentage of full-time faculty members teaching evening classes. Final authority to hire faculty lies with academic departments. Some

full-time faculty members teach exclusively in the evening.
No regular faculty meetings are held. Faculty members are
reimbursed for non-credit teaching; this policy is under consideration for revision.

V. Scheduling

Each academic department is responsible for the class
schedule. The Dean does not have the authority to revise
the class schedule. Courses giving three hours of credit are
scheduled two nights a week. Cleveland College is presently
researching the mature woman student who has returned to
the classroom after an absence of several years. The "Dismissed" student is also being researched in order to determine failure factors. Adult students have an overall higher
grade point average than comparable undergraduates of the
18-22 age group. Part-time evening students are eligible for
the Dean's List with 15 hours and a 3.20 average on a 4.00
scale.

VI. General

An active student council holds membership in a number of university committees and participates in discussions
regarding the academic program. A new Freshman Studies
Program has just been introduced. In general, all evening
divisions are not receiving adequate support. The Dean of
Cleveland College of Case Western Reserve University is responsible to the President.

VII. Student Recruitment

Newspaper, radio and television publicity are used.
Special motivational appeals have been developed for industry and civic organizations.

* * *

Columbia University
New York, New York
School of General Studies

Total enrollment 17,531   Private Institution
(grad and undergrad)   Semester System

I. Admission Policies

Deadline for application for admission for evening students is about one month prior to registration. "Special" students may take courses if they have a Bachelor's degree or are matriculated and in good standing at another college. Admission requirements are high school graduation or equivalent, test scores and personal interviews. Non-matriculating students must maintain a "B" average; regular students must maintain a "C" average. The special degree for adults is the Bachelor of Science with an enrollment of 3, 200. Admission policies are set by the Faculty Admissions Committee. Day and evening students may enroll in the same classes. There is an orientation for evening students.

II. Terminology

Title of Division: School of General Studies, defined: A degree, liberal arts oriented school.

III. Fees

There is no fee differential between day and evening classes. Refunds are made if withdrawal is done by the last day of course change period.

IV. Faculty and Faculty Recruitment

80% teaching evening courses are full-time. Final authority to hire faculty lies with the academic departments. The Dean of the School of General Studies can reject a faculty member assigned to teach eving classes. Overloads for faculty members are not permitted.

V. Scheduling

The Dean of the School of General Studies is responsible for the evening class schedule. Three credit hour courses are scheduled two nights a week. Day and evening classes are equal in terms of quality. Part-time evening students are eligible for the Dean's List with 9 points in 3 different subjects of Liberal Arts only with 13. 1 average.

Columbia Univ. (cont.)

VI. General

Two students participate in discussions regarding the academic program on the Committee on Instruction--The policy board for curriculum. In general, all evening divisions are not receiving adequate support. The Dean of the School of General Studies is responsible to the Provost.

Community College of Baltimore
Evening Division

Total enrollment 3, 400	Public Institution
Evening enrollment 1, 700	Semester System

I. Admission Policies

Students may register without prior application during the week before classes begin and with a penalty during the first week of classes. No transcripts are required for registration. There is no limit to the amount of work taken as non-matriculating students. Regular admission requirements are high school graduation or equivalent and special interest in a certain field of study. A student who has failed half or more of his load, or has attempted 27 college credits and has earned less than a cumulative quality point average of 1. 5 or who has attempted 42 college credits and has earned less than a cumulative quality point average of 1. 7, will be subject to academic review. Admission policies are set by the Administrative Council of the College. Day students may enroll in evening classes if they are unable to schedule those classes during the day; evening students may register for day classes after day students' registration. Orientation for evening students is held each semester.

II. Terminology

Title of Division: Evening Division of the Community College of Baltimore, defined: A Division of the college offering similar programs with the same standards as regular day courses on a part-time basis.

III. Fees

Refunds are based on individual courses and a graduated percentage system.

IV. Faculty and Faculty Recruitment

Five percent of the faculty teaching Evening Division classes are full-time staff members with major responsibility in the day. Final authority to hire Evening Division faculty lies with the Associate Dean for the Evening Division. Regular faculty meetings are held at the beginning of each semester. Full-time day faculty members are not assigned overload classes in the Evening Division except on an emergency basis. The exception to this rule is the use of day school laboratory assistants in the evening.

V. Scheduling

The Associate Dean for the Evening Division is responsible for the evening class schedule. Three credit hour classes are scheduled one night a week. Part-time evening students are not eligible for the Dean's List but a special "Honor Roll" is compiled for evening division students based on number of credits earned and grades.

VI. General

The evening division is receiving adequate support. The Associate Dean for the Evening Division is responsible to the President of the College.

VII. Student Recruitment

Newspaper advertisement and news releases, radio spots, public service television programs, and special posters are main avenues utilized in addition to extensive mailing lists for brochures. Special newsprint supplements and other mailings with specific appeals are also used.

* * *

C. W. Post College
Long Island, New York
Evening and Extension Division
Total enrollment 3,500 (day)   Private Institution
        2,500 (grad)   Semester System
Evening enrollment 1,700

I. Admission Policies

There is no deadline for application for admission to evening classes prior to registration. Non-matriculated students may register for credit courses without transcripts and may take a maximum of 30 semester hours. Admission requirements are high school graduation or equivalent or acceptable college transcripts. Mail registration is used. Students are dismissed after completing six semester hours below 2.0 on a 4.0 scale. A special degree for adults is being considered. Admission policies are set by the Dean of the Evening Division in consultation with the Admissions Office. Day and evening students may enroll in the same classes. There is no orientation for evening students; it takes place during a personal interview with advisors.

II. Terminology

Title of Division: Evening and Extension Division of C. W. Post College, defined: Comprises all adult undergraduate students enrolled at C. W. Post College and at its extension. It also includes all non-credit Continuing Education Programs.

III. Fees

Tuition for day and evening classes are the same because the courses are exactly the same. Registration fees for evening students are less than day because evening students are unable to fully utilize all college facilities.

IV. Faculty and Faculty Recruitment

50% teaching evening classes are full-time. Final authority to hire evening faculty lies with the Dean of the College. Some full-time faculty members teach exclusively

98

in the evening. Regular evening faculty meetings are not held. Faculty members are discouraged from teaching courses on an overload basis but may teach non-credit courses with no objections.

V. Scheduling

The Dean is responsible for reviewing the evening class schedule and making revisions and recommendations as he sees fit. Three credit hour courses are scheduled two nights a week. Part-time evening students are eligible for the Dean's List after completing 12 semester hours with a 3.5 average.

VI. General

Students participate in discussion regarding the academic program through the school newspaper and the honor society, Alpha Sigma Lambda. In general, all evening divisions are not receiving adequate support. The Dean of the Evening Division is responsible to the Dean of the College. Audio-visual instructional aids are available for evening classes.

VII. Student Recruitment

Newspaper and radio publicity are used. Special motivational appeals have been developed for industry in the form of personal letters and by membership in the Association for Training and Development.

* * *

DePaul University

Total enrollment 9,878   Church-related Institution
Evening enrollment 6,034   Quarter System

I. Admission Policies

Deadline for admission, four weeks prior to registration. Students may register for credit courses without transcripts. 40 quarter hours limit for non-matriculating students. Admission requirements are good standing at previous college attended, high school graduation in upper half of

99

DePaul University (cont.)

class. Mail registration is used. Students must maintain no less than a 2.00 average. ACT or other tests required if less than one year of college work has been completed and the student intends to obtain a degree. A special degree program is being considered. Admissions policies are set by the Admissions Office for regular students; by deans of various colleges for special students. No more than one third of an evening class may be populated by day students.

II. Terminology

Each college has its own evening division, but the evening liberal arts bears the name University College. Continuing Education, defined: Education sought by someone for reason of employment benefits, thirst for knowledge, etc.

III. Fees

Tuition: 12-14 credit hours--$450; part-time evening $25 per credit hour; part-time day, $37 per credit hour. Refunds are made according to withdrawal date.

IV. Faculty and Faculty Recruitment

40% of the evening faculty are full-time faculty. Authority to hire faculty lies with Deans in charge of the division. Annual faculty meetings are held with entire staff and periodic meetings with departments.

V. Scheduling

A director of the evening division is responsible for the schedule. Four credit hour classes are held either one or two nights a week. Part-time students are eligible for the Dean's list with a 3.0 average for 36 credit hours of work.

VI. General

In general, evening divisions are receiving adequate support. The Directors are immediately responsible to the Dean of the College to which he is assigned. All Colleges have a Director of Continuing Education or Evening Division. The usual audio-visual aids are available.

VII. Student Recruitment

Newspaper and radio publicity are used. Public Relations--Special motivational appeals have been developed for industry and organizations such as the Chamber of Commerce.

* * *

University of Denver
Continuing Education
Denver, Colorado

Total enrollment 8, 926, non-credit 735	Private, Church-related Institution
Evening enrollment 2, 922, non-credit 735	Quarter System

I. Admission Policies

Deadline for application for admission to evening classes is about one month prior to registration. Students are registered provisionally before transcripts are submitted. Non-matriculated students may take a maximum of 15 quarter hours. Admission requirements are twenty-one years of age or those who have recently attended another college but are not eligible for admission. Other students may take such credit courses as their previous study of experience qualified them to take. All degree candidates must maintain a "C" average to remain in good standing. There is no special degree for adults. Admission policies are set by the faculties of the respective colleges. Day and evening students may enroll in the same classes. There is no orientation program for evening students. The policy of the University is to encourage unclassified students enrolled in credit courses to matriculate.

II. Terminology

Title of Division: Office of Continuing Education, defined: Continuing Education as used at the University of Denver implies non-credit courses and programs. It is defined as educational opportunities offered for anyone whose chief occupation or role in life is no longer that of a full-time student. This definition applies to both credit and non-credit programs.

University of Denver (cont.)

III. Fees

There is no fee differential between day and evening classes. Refunds are based on a diminishing percentage formula which extends through the third week of classes. No limit is set on the extent of withdrawal (one, two or three courses, etc.).

IV. Faculty and Faculty Recruitment

75% teaching evening classes are full-time faculty members. The deans of the respective colleges hire all faculty members who teach credit courses at night. No regular faculty meetings are held. Overloads involving the teaching of both credit and non-credit courses are discouraged by the University's administration. Special permission must be obtained for a full-time faculty member to participate in a non-credit activity.

V. Scheduling

The deans of the respective colleges are responsible for the scheduling of evening credit courses. The Office of Continuing Education prepares the schedule of non-credit courses and programs. Three credit hour courses are scheduled both one and two nights a week, depending on the subject. The Office of Continuing Education of the University of Denver plans to cooperate with other schools in the Denver area on a project sponsored by the Adult Education Council of Metropolitan Denver which obtains information on enrollment trends. Day and evening classes are equal in terms of quality since the same faculty teach both. Part-time evening students are not eligible for the Dean's List.

VI. General

The deans of each college have a student advisory council which meets regularly and participates in discussion regarding the academic program. Law students are participating as recorders and advisors for Model City Resident Committees. In general, all evening divisions are not receiving adequate support. The Coordinator of the Office of Continuing Education is responsible to the Vice-Chancellor for Academic Affairs.   Audio-visual aids are available for evening classes.

VII.   Student Recruitment

Newspaper, radio and television publicity are used. Special motivational appeals have been developed for industry and other civic organizations.

*   *   *

Drake   University
Des Moines, Iowa
University College

| Total enrollment 5,000 | Private Institution |
| Evening enrollment 2,500 | Semester System |

I.   Admission Policies

A student may register for credit courses without transcripts but is limited to a maximum of 30 semester hours in the non-matriculated status.   Admission requirements for non-matriculating students are high school graduation or equivalent and a probable chance of success; regular students must meet the regular admission requirements for the University.   Students must maintain a 2.0 or "C" average or better; one or two semesters of probation are permitted. Admission policies are set by the University Admissions Committee.   Day and evening students may enroll in the same classes in some cases with approval of their advisors. Youthful students are encouraged to apply for admission befor starting their program, while more mature students usually matriculate after accumulating some credits.

II.   Terminology

Title of Division: University College--Center for Continuing Education, defined: University College is one of nine colleges which offers evening, Saturday, and extension classes.   Center for Continuing Education develops program with business, industry, community service, and other groups of a non-credit nature.   Continuing Education is a series of learning situations aimed at solving problems recognized by the learner as needing solutions.   This includes both formal and informal experiences moving a person from where he is in the direction of some desired goal.

Drake University (cont.)

III. Fees

Evening classes are $6.00 per semester hour less than day classes. Refunds are based on a diminishing scale of 90% for the first week to 0% after five weeks.

IV. Faculty and Faculty Recruitment

60% teaching evening classes are full time. Final authority to hire evening faculty lies jointly with the Dean of University College and the Dean of the teaching college. The Dean of University College has the authority to reject a faculty member assigned to teach evening classes. Full-time faculty members teaching only in the evening are responsible to their college deans, respectively. Overloads are permitted for all faculty members if it does not interfere with the full and effective performance of the individual's responsibility to the University.

V. Scheduling

The Dean of University College is responsible for the evening class schedule, and has the authority to revise it. Three credit hour classes are scheduled both one and two nights a week. Day and evening classes are equal in terms of quality. Part-time students are not eligible for the Dean's List.

VI. General

Some courses for economically deprived populations are planned. Students are included on all university committees and the Senate. The evening division is receiving adequate support. The Dean of University College is responsible to the Provost. Audio-visual instructional aids are available for evening classes.

VII. Student Recruitment

Newspaper, radio and television publicity are used. Special motivational appeals have been developed for industry in the form of posters, schedules and brochures and also for Civic Organizations.

* * *

Drexel Institute of Technology
Evening College

Total enrollment 11,025   Private Institution
Evening enrollment 2,879 under.   Quarter System
1,500 grad.

104

I. Admission Policies

Deadline for application for admission is approximately six weeks prior to registration. Students may not register for credit courses without transcripts. Admission requirement for non-matriculating students is bachelor's degree; regular students must be high school graduates and show satisfactory performance on qualification test. A 2.0 quality point average is required for graduation; non-degree students must complete each course satisfactorily. Admission policies are set by the Admissions Committee of the Evening College. Day and evening students may register in the same classes with permission of their respective deans. Orientation for evening students is on registration day.

II. Terminology

Title of Division: Evening College, defined: Completely autonomous under program of studies offered after 6 p. m.

III. Fees

Evening students pay $25 per quarter hour plus annual institute fee of $35; part-time day students pay $45 per quarter hour plus institute fee of $30, $50 or $70, depending on credit carried or quarter of study. No cash refunds are made; tuition credit of 75% is given if withdrawal is in first two weeks of class, 50% in third and fourth weeks, 25% in fifth and sixth week, none after the sixth week.

IV. Faculty and Faculty Recruitment

25% teaching evening classes are full-time in Business Administration and 15% over all. Final authority for hiring evening faculty lies with the Dean of the Evening College. General faculty meetings are held yearly and department meetings as often as necessary. Faculty members are permitted to teach on an overload basis a maximum of two evenings per week at three periods per evening.

V. Scheduling

The Dean of the Evening College is responsible for

Drexel Institute of Technology (cont.)

the evening schedule. Three credit hour classes are scheduled one night a week. Part-time evening students are eligible for the Dean's List after completing 6 1/2 quarter
hours with a 3.5 quality point average.

VI. General

Day students participate more in discussions regarding the academic program than evening students. Much emphasis is placed on leadership development through co-cur-
ricular and extra-curricular activities. The evening division
is receiving adequate support. The Dean of the Evening College is responsible to the Vice-President for Academic Affairs and directly to the President in major decisions. Most
audio-visual instructional aids are available for evening
classes.

VII. Student Recruitment

Newspaper publicity is used. Special motivational appeals have been developed for industry and professional organizations.

* * *

Drury College
Adult Education
Springfield, Missouri
Total enrollment 2, 462   Private Institution
Evening enrollment 1, 294

I. Admission Policies

All students must be registered by the first night of
classes. Students may register for credit courses without
transcripts. Non-matriculated students may take 8 hours a
semester to a total of 94 hours before matriculation is required. Admission requirements are completion of registration cards and admissibility to previous college attended.
Mail registration is used. Students must maintain at least
a 2.0 after a total of 12 semester hours or they are placed
on scholastic probation. A special degree for adults is offered: The Bachelor of Science Degree, with an enrollment
of 180 per semester. Admission requirements for the spe-

cial degree are previous transcripts on file; 2.0 average
overall required; admission test scores should be good. Admission policies are set by the Adult Education Council.
Day and evening students do not usually register for the same
classes. Orientation is held at the beginning of each semester.

II. Terminology

Title of Division: Adult Education Division, defined:
A program for adults 18 years of age or older not in full-
time school. --For individuals who cannot pursue an educational program in the regular session of the college. The
program will provide stimulus and leadership in the cultural
and intellectual life of the surrounding community.

III. Fees

Evening fees are set by the credit hour; day fees are
by semester to cover 12 to 16 semester hours. Refunds are
made on a graduating percentage basis.

IV. Faculty and Faculty Recruitment

15% teaching evening classes are full-time faculty
members. Final authority to hire faculty lies with the Adult
Education Council. The Director of the Adult Education Division may reject a faculty member assigned to teach evening classes. Some full-time faculty members teach exclusively in the evening and they are responsible to the Director of the Adult Education Division. Part-time faculty members meet once each semester. Day division faculty members are permitted to teach one assignment on an overload
basis per semester.

V. Scheduling

The Director of the Adult Education Division is responsible for the evening class schedule. The Schedule of
Evening Classes is planned by the Director and he has authority to revise it. Individual courses are scheduled for
one night a week with the division operating four nights. Day
and evening classes are equal in terms of quality but different in instructional methods. Part-time evening students are

Drury College (cont.)

eligible for the Dean's List with at least eight hours a semester with a grade point average of 3.3 or higher.

VI. General

A student council is being organized in order for students to participate in discussions regarding the academic program. TV courses for credit are offered on commercial stations. The Residential Center is ninety miles from campus. The Director of the Adult Education Division is responsible to the President of the College. Audio-visual instructional aids are available for evening classes.

VII. Student Recruitment

Newspaper, radio and television publicity are used. Special motivational appeals have been developed for industry and civic organizations.

* * *

Dutchess Community College
Poughkeepsie, New York
Office of Continuing Education

Total enrollment 3,799   Public Institution
Evening enrollment 1,891   Semester System

I. Admission Policies

There is no deadline for admission to the College as a part-time student prior to the start of class. Students may register for credit courses without transcripts. There is no limit to the amount of work taken as non-matriculated students. Admission requirements for regular students are acceptable college transcripts or high school graduation or equivalency. Mail registration is used. There is no special degree for adults. Admission policies are established by the College administration. Day and evening students may register in the same classes. There is no orientation for evening students.

108

II. Terminology

Title of Division: Office of Continuing Education, defined: Educational opportunities for area residents whose daily responsibilities prevent them from attending the College's day division as full-time students and who seek to complete initial higher educational objectives, update skills and techniques, and seek cultural enrichment.

III. Fees

Part-time students pay a $3 college fee; full-time students pay a $25 college fee. Refunds are made on a graduating percentage basis.

IV. Faculty and Faculty Recruitment

55% teaching evening classes are full time. Final authority for hiring faculty lies with the Dean of Continuing Education. Regularly scheduled faculty meetings are held evenings. When faculty members teach on an overload basis, they are compensated for expenses incurred.

V. Scheduling

The Dean of Continuing Education is responsible for the evening class schedule, and has the authority to revise it. Three credit hour courses are scheduled one night a week. Day and evening classes are equal in terms of quality. Part-time evening students are eligible for the Dean's List based on all courses taken while completing the last 12 semester hours with a GPA of 3.2 or better.

VI. General

Students participate in discussion regarding the academic program through the Evening Student Association. The evening division is receiving adequate support. The Dean of Continuing Education is responsible to the President. Complete audio-visual instructional aids are available for evening classes, including closed circuit television.

Dutchess Community College (cont.)

VII. Student Recruitment

Newspaper, radio and television publicity are used. Special motivational appeals have been developed for industry and civic organizations.

* * *

East Tennessee State University
Continuing Education
Johnson City, Tennessee

Total enrollment 8,500   Public Institution
Evening enrollment 2,500   Quarter System

I. Admission Policies

Deadline for application for admission to evening classes is two weeks prior to registration; however, this deadline is not enforced. Registration process will not be considered complete if a student registers before transcripts are submitted. Non-matriculated students may register for credit work but they are cautioned that credit is not applied toward a degree unless approved by the appropriate college dean when they do matriculate. Freshmen must maintain a grade point average of 1.5; sophomores 1.8; juniors 2.0. There is no special degree program for adults; one is being considered in accounting and industrial education. Admission policies are set by the Dean of Admissions. Day and evening students may enroll in the same classes with approval. There is no orientation for evening students. Everything within reason is done to maintain evening degree programs that are an integral part of the total University.

II. Terminology

Title of Division: School of Continuing Education, defined: A division through which educational services of the University are extended to individuals and groups other than day students. Includes both credit and non-credit programs.

III. Fees

There is no fee differential between day and evening

110

classes. Refunds are made only if classes are cancelled. Students withdrawing from all classes receive refunds according to a published schedule.

IV. Faculty and Faculty Recruitment

75-90% teaching evening classes are full-time faculty members. Final authority to hire faculty lies with the President upon recommendation by the Dean of the School of Continuing Education. Some full-time faculty members teach exclusively in the evening and are responsible to the Dean of the School of Continuing Education. Faculty meetings are held with certain groups. No teaching overloads are permitted.

V. Scheduling

The Dean of the School of Continuing Education is responsible for the evening class schedule and has the authority to revise it. Three credit hour courses are scheduled both one and two nights a week. A study is planned to compare day and evening classes, procedures and results. Part-time evening students are eligible for the Dean's List with a 3.5 after carrying 14 quarter hours.

VI. General

Students are invited to suggest additions or modifications of academic programs. There is a Center at Kingsport which is shared with the University of Tennessee. The evening division is receiving adequate support. The Dean of the School of Continuing Education is responsible to the Dean of University Faculty and the President of the University. Complete audio-visual instructional aids are available at each Center of the University.

VII. Student Recruitment

Newspaper, radio and television publicity are used. Special motivational appeals have been developed for industry and various civic organizations.

* * *

111

University of Georgia
Georgia Center for Continuing Education
Total enrollment 17,000   State Land Grant Public
Evening enrollment: Institution
   416 on campus, credit   Quarter System
   538 off campus, credit
   600 non-credit

I. Admission Policies

Deadline for application for admission to evening
classes is about two weeks prior to registration. Transcripts are required of all students except transient, special
auditing, and refresher course students. Transient students
must provide "letter of permission and good standing" from
their respective deans. Auditing students sign a "Personal
Improvement Only" form. While Athens Evening Classes students may earn a major portion of Bachelor of Arts and
Bachelor of Business Education degree credits in evening
classes, off-campus center students are limited to one-fourth
of degree requirements. Admission requirements are 16
high school units or GED, CEEB scores of 700 plus, good
standing at previous college attended, and residence within
commuting distance. Students must maintain an average of
seventy or be placed on probation. Students are dismissed
after second consecutive probation or a quarter average below sixty. Admission policies are established largely by the
University Admissions Committee, with a degree of flexibility in policy left to the discretion of Center for Continuing
Education administration. Day and evening students may
register in the same classes with permission. Students receive an individual orientation during application interview
for evening courses.

II. Terminology

Title of Division: Center for Continuing Education.
Continuing Education, as defined at the University of Georgia,
includes both credit and non-credit courses offered to adults
whose primary occupation is other than that of full-time students. It is a service provided for adults who are seeking
to improve themselves personally and professionally in order
to keep abreast of the world in which they live.

112

III. Fees

The basic fee is $8.00 per quarter hour. There is
no refund for reductions of load, but students who drop out
in first four weeks are awarded a percentage refund. Evening students do not pay application, health and student activity fees.

IV. Faculty and Faculty Recruitment

20% of evening classes are taught by regular full-time
faculty members on an overload basis. Final authority to
hire faculty members lies jointly with the administration of
the Center for Continuing Education and other University administrators. No regular faculty meetings are held. Regular University faculty members may teach one quarter and
during the summer on an overload basis.

V. Scheduling

The Director of evening classes is responsible for the
schedule of classes and has the authority to make changes in
it. However, he seeks the advice of academic department
heads. Five-quarter hour courses are scheduled two nights
a week.

VI. General

The evening division is not receiving adequate support
in comparison with the day program. Some departments
within the University realistically recognize their role in adult
education. Response ranges from complete cooperation to
mild interest. The Director of Athens Evening Classes is
responsible to the Assistant Director of Continuing Education
in charge of University Extension. Audio-visual instructional aids are available for use in evening classes. Part-time
evening students are not eligible for the Dean's List.

VII. Student Recruitment

Community newspapers support adult evening classes
with news releases, as do local radio stations. Industry is
encouraged to participate financially in order to assist their

113

University of Georgia (cont.)

employees in becoming students. Church groups also reach some lower socio-economic groups to encourage college education. Extensive mailings are made of brochures announcing course schedules. Evening class students recruit many new students.

* * *

Harvard University
(University Extension)
Cambridge, Mass.

Semester System   Private Institution

I. Admission Policies

There is no deadline for application for admission to classes taken through university extension. Students may register for credit courses before transcripts are submitted. A few Extension students are admitted as "special" students to the Faculty of Arts and Sciences and take some of their work in regular day courses. There is no limit to the amount of work taken as non-matriculating students. Students may apply for admission to candidacy for the degree of Bachelor of Arts in Extension Studies on one of the following bases: a) those who have had no previous college work must satisfactorily complete the equivalent of one year of college work--four full courses or eight half-courses--under the Commission on Extension Courses, or in the Harvard Summer School. When the student is admitted to the degree, these courses count retroactively, b) those who have had previous college work and wish to have it evaluated for possible transfer credit must satisfactorily complete two full courses or four half-courses under the Commission on Extension Courses, or in the summer school, before presenting official transcripts of this work. College catalogues for the years attended must be supplied also. According to the Director: "We have a very informal structure as far as admission to degree candidacy and rate of progress toward the degree is concerned. I can't recall in my experience that anyone was dropped permanently for academic reasons." Admission policies are set by the Administrative Board for University Extension. Day students do not receive credit for extension courses. No orientation program is used for extension students.

114

II. Terminology

Title of Division: University Extension (within the Faculty of Arts and Sciences).

III. Fees

There is a fee differential between day and extension classes.   No course fees (tuition, laboratory, conference or credit) will be refunded after October 18 for fall term and through-year courses, or after February 21 for spring term courses.   The basic tuition is $5 per term.

IV. Faculty and Faculty Recruitment

All instructors in University Extension are "part-time," but are normally full-time in their day faculties.   The Director of University Extension invites them to teach and the approval of the program each year, including the instructors, is given by the faculty of Arts and Sciences at Harvard University.   Ordinarily, a reception is held for the faculty annually.

V. Scheduling

The Director of University Extension is responsible for the scheduling of classes.   Classes are normally held one evening per week.   Students attending part-time are not eligible for the Dean's List.

VI. General

Students discuss the academic program with their instructors.   Harvard University has been offering television courses for credit for the past ten years.   Nine television courses will be offered over two television stations each term this year for credit.   These courses are prepared with the support of the U.S. Navy as part of the PACE Program of college-level instruction.   The administration recognizes the need and importance of the program in adult education.   The Director of University Extension is responsible to the Dean of the Faculty of Arts and Sciences.

VII. Student Recruitment

Some publicity is given to the courses offered through University Extension in newspapers and through radio and television.

* * *

Hofstra University
University College

Total enrollment 8, 000
  undergraduate
Evening enrollment 2, 000
  undergraduate

Private Institution
Semester System

I. Admission Policies

Deadline for application for admission is about one week prior to the start of the semester. Students may register for credit courses without transcripts but they must be received by the end of the semester. Admission requirements are high school graduation or GED and advisement test or satisfactory record from previously attended colleges. Students may register by mail only if a formal plan of studies has been worked out for them. The student receives a copy of it for reference when filling out the mail registration forms. Students must maintain a 2.0 in order to remain in school. A special degree for adults is not offered or considered. Admission policies are set by the Dean of University College with Faculty Admission Committee and the Director of Admissions. Day and evening students may enroll in the same classes. Orientation for evening students is held at the beginning of each semester.

II. Terminology

Title of Division: University College (credit program); The Institute for Community Education (non-credit). Defined: College of the University offering programs and courses for adults. Continuing Education is any involvement of adults in education--undergraduate, graduate, credit and non-credit work; workshops, conferences, seminars, etc.

III. Fees

Refunds are made based on the date of withdrawal.

IV. Faculty and Faculty Recruitment

60% teaching evening classes are full time. The final
authority to hire part-time evening faculty lies with Department Chairmen with final approval of the Dean of University
College. Faculty members are responsible to the Department Chairmen and the Dean. Faculty members are permitted to teach three credits on an overload basis; non-
credit courses are subject to department chairman's approval.

V. Scheduling

The Dean of University College is responsible for the
evening class schedule. Three credit hour classes are
scheduled two nights a week. Part-time students are not
eligible for the Dean's List; there is a special Honor's List
for part-time students, which is annual and based on a minimum of twelve credits with a 3.3 average.

VI. General

Students are being selected for participation on all
faculty committees in order to take part in discussions regarding the academic program. The evening division is receiving adequate support except in the area of scholarships.
The Dean of University College is responsible to the Provost.

VII. Student Recruitment

Newspaper advertisements and feature stories are
used. Special motivational appeals have been developed by a
number of methods: Participation in community and county
career and education clinics, talks to various groups, group
information sessions; College-for-a-day program for adults.

*   *   *

University of Illinois
Division of University Extension
Total enrollment 31,000   Public Institution
Evening enrollment (Extra-   Semester System
mural Division 12,000)

I. Admission Policies

Deadline for application for admission for fall and
spring semester is by the fourth class; for the Summer session is by the first class.   Registration for a degree candi-
date is not complete without a transcript.   Non-degree students may take an unlimited amount of semester hours.   Admission requirements: 18 years of age or high school graduate and must meet prerequisites.   Mail registration is used:
application forms are issued to students at the first class
meeting, the student completes it and mails it with tuition
fees to Admissions Office.   There is no special degree program for adults.

II. Terminology

Title of Division: Division of University Extension,
defined: A Division which extends campus resources off
campus but is not an evening college.   Continuing Education,
defined: "Any process by which men or women (either alone
or in groups) try to improve themselves by increasing their
skill, their knowledge, or their sensitivity; or the process
by which individuals or organizations try to improve men or
women in these ways." (Cy Houle).

III. Fees

Extramural students usually are taking only one course
and are assessed $15 per semester hour.   Refunds are
made based on the date of withdrawal.

IV. Faculty and Faculty Recruitment

95% teaching extramural classes are full-time faculty
members.   Final authority to hire evening faculty lies with
the Chairman of Department and Dean of Extension.   Some
full-time faculty members teach exclusively in the evening.
Regular faculty meetings are held as needed.   Faculty members are encouraged to teach special credit and non-credit

courses, to participate in institutes, seminars and conferences.

V. Scheduling

The on-campus evening class schedule is not compiled by the Dean of the Division of University Extension. Extramural classes are developed in consultation with academic departments. Three credit hour classes are scheduled one night a week.

VI. General

Some courses are planned in off-campus locations for economically deprived populations. In general, all evening divisions are not receiving adequate support. The Director of Extramural Classes is responsible to the Dean of the Division of University Extension who reports to the President. Audiovisual instructional aids are available for all classes.

VII. Student Recruitment

Newspaper and radio publicity are used. Special motivational appeals have been developed for industry and civic organizations.

* * *

Indiana Central College
Evening and Graduate Division

Total enrollment 2,393   Church-related Liberal
Evening enrollment 1,257   Arts Coll.
                                   Semester System

I. Admission Policies

There is a deadline for admission to evening classes; students may not register for credit courses without transcripts. Non-matriculating students may take a maximum of thirty hours. Admission requirements are high school graduation and successful completion of the SAT tests. Mail registration is used. Students must maintain a "C" average at the end of first two enrollments. A special degree program is not offered and not considered. Admission policies are set by the College Administration and Faculty. Some classes are mixed with day and evening students. There is

119

Indiana Central College (cont.)

no orientation.

II. Terminology

Evening Division: An administrative term used to distinguish between the day and evening programs. Continuing Education, defined: Credit and non-credit college level work offered for those actively engaged in work or other full-time pursuits.

III. Fees

The Evening Division fees are less than day school. No refunds made on tuition two weeks after classes begin.

IV. Faculty and Faculty Recruitment

33% teaching evening classes are full-time. Final authority to hire full-time faculty lies with the Academic Dean; part-time faculty, Evening Division Dean. Regular faculty meetings are held annually. Faculty is permitted to teach one overload course.

V. Scheduling

The Dean of the Evening Division is responsible for the schedule. Class schedules compiled on the basis of regular rotation and special need. Three credit hour classes are held one night a week, four and five hour classes meet twice. Part-time evening students are eligible for the Dean's List after completing 15 hours with a 10.5.

VI. General

The Master's degree program in the area of Liberal Arts is offered in the evening. The Evening Division is receiving adequate support. The Dean of the Evening Division is directly responsible to the President of the College. Audio-visual aids such as films and film strips are used in instruction.

VII.   Student Recruitment

Newspaper, radio and television publicity are used.
Public Relations: Special motivational appeals have been developed for industry and organizations such as the Chamber
of Commerce and the Kiwanis and Rotarians.

* * *

Iona College
New Rochelle, New York
Division of Business Administration

Total enrollment 3, 223   Private Institution
Evening Enrollment 856   Semester System
Undergraduate enrollment 260

I. Admission Policies

Deadline for application for admission to evening
classes is about one month prior to registration.   Students
may not register for credit courses without transcripts.   Students may not take courses without being matriculated unless
they have a letter of permission from their college.   Admission requirements for regular students are high school graduation and college board scores.   Mail registration is not
used.   Students must maintain a "C" average.   There is no
special degree for adults.   Admission policies are set by the
Committee on Administration.   Day and evening students may
enroll in the same classes.   There is no orientation for evening students.

II.   Terminology

Title of Division: Division of Business Administration, defined: It refers to the fact that a B. B. A. degree is
offered in the evening.

III.   Fees

Day students pay a "flat" tuition rate; evening students
are charged by the semester hour.   Refunds are made on a
graduating percentage basis.

121

Iona College (cont.)

IV. Faculty and Faculty Recruitment

90% teaching evening classes are full-time. Final
authority to hire evening faculty lies with the Director of the
Division of Business Administration in cooperation with the
Chairman of the Department. Overloads for faculty members are not permitted.

V. Scheduling

The Director of the Division of Business Administration is responsible for the evening class schedule and has the
authority to revise it. Three credit hour courses are scheduled two nights a week. Day and evening classes are equal
in terms of quality. Part-time evening students are eligible
for the Dean's List with a 3.4.

VI. General

Students participate in discussions regarding the academic program through membership on certain College Committees. The evening division is receiving adequate support.
The Director of the Division of Business Administration is
responsible to the Dean of the Day school.

VII. Student Recruitment

Newspaper and radio publicity are used. Special
motivational appeals have been developed for industry and
civic organizations.

* * *

Iowa State University
Ames, Iowa
University Extension

Total enrollment 18,200   Public, land-grant insti-
Evening enrollment --   tution
  (no figure given)   Quarter System

I. Admission Policies

Applicants for admission must submit the required
applications for admission and the necessary official tran-

122

scripts to the Admissions Office at least 10 days prior to the beginning of the orientation. A student may register for credit courses without transcripts only as a "restricted non-degree" student. "Special" students may take an unlimited number of hours for credit--the "special" student is considered a student who is not working towards a degree and who takes classes on a "sporadic" basis and is highly selective. Admission requirements for regular students: a certificate of high school credits, including a complete statement of the applicant's high school record, rank in class, scores on standardized tests, and certification of graduation. Applicant normally must be in upper half of his graduating class. Mail registration is used. Retention policy: must maintain a 2.0 average. Admission policies for evening students are the same as for regular students. Day and evening students may enroll in the same classes. No orientation program is held for evening students.

II.   Terminology

Title of Division: Extension Courses and Conferences as a Department of University Extension. Defined: Administration and Supervision of all off-campus credit courses, and some off-campus non-credit classes and on-campus non-credit conferences, workshops, etc. Adult education implies --"Quantitative educational experiences as a vital part of continuing education, i.e., learning new skills, up-dating old ones, new techniques, etc. Qualitative educational experiences are the second part of any Continuing Educational definition; i.e., personal development, growth and maturity. This can involve both positive and negative influences on us as individual members of society."

III.   Fees

Day and evening students pay the same fees. Refund policies: Ten percent of the total fee will be deducted for each class meeting attended through the fifth class meeting. No refund will be made if a student withdraws after the fifth class meeting.

IV.   Faculty and Faculty Recruitment

There is no policy regarding the percentage of evening faculty members that must be full-time faculty. No

Iowa State University (cont.)

full-time faculty members teach exclusively in the evening.
No strict policy exists for faculty member teaching an over-
load--some faculty receive payment on an overload basis.

V. Scheduling

Departments are responsible for the evening class
schedule. The schedule is compiled through the admissions
office. Day and evening classes are equal in quality. Part-
time students are not eligible for the Dean's List.

VI. General

Most departments have student representatives on various departmental committees so that students have the opportunity to participate in discussions of the academic program.
The Leader of Extension Courses and Conferences reports to
the Dean of University Extension.

VII. Student Recruitment

Special newspaper ads and news stories are used for
publicity purposes, as well as radio and television announcements. Contact is made with business and industry and with
various civic clubs and organizations concerning special
courses and programs offered by the University Extension.

* * *

The Johns Hopkins University
Baltimore, Maryland
Evening College
Total enrollment 11, 800   Private Institution
Evening enrollment 7, 500   Semester System

I. Admission Policies

There is no deadline for application for admission--
applications are not accepted unless they can be processed
before registration. Undergraduate students may register for
credit courses without transcripts. There is no limit to the
amount of work taken as non-matriculated students; only 16

credits taken under this status may be applied toward a certificate or degree. Admission requirements are high school graduation, in good standing at previous college attended and they must meet specific course prerequisites. Mail registration is used. Students must maintain satisfactory academic and conduct records. All records are reviewed each term by the Academic Standing Committee. There are special certificate and degree programs for adults on the undergraduate and graduate level. Admission policies are set by the Advisory Board of the Evening College. Day and evening students do not enroll for the same classes, because the programs are basically different and are constructed for the particular public they serve. There is no orientation for evening students.

II. Terminology

Title of Division: Evening College, defined: A program of part-time higher education for adults. Emphasis is placed on work toward certificates and degrees.

III. Fees

Tuition is $30 per semester credit in the evening and $80 per contact hour during the day (part-time). No refunds are made once classes have begun.

IV. Faculty and Faculty Recruitment

Approximately 40% teaching evening classes are full-time. Final authority to hire evening faculty lies with the Dean of the Evening College. No full-time faculty members teach exclusively in the evening. Regular faculty meetings are held with many groups of the faculty usually in the fall. Faculty members who teach courses on an overload basis are paid accordingly but are not requested to teach more than one course per term during the academic year.

V. Scheduling

The Dean of the Evening College is responsible for the evening class schedule. The Dean has the authority to revise the evening class schedule. Three credit hour classes are scheduled both one and two nights per week. "The day and

evening programs are different, and they are offered for
very different publics. The basic philosophy is quite different for the two programs. We think and hope that both programs are of very high quality." There is no Dean's List.

VI. General

Some surveys are done from time to time which en-
able students to participate in discussion regarding the academic programs. The Evening College program is essentially one offering credit courses to be applied toward degrees and certificates, graduate programs are being stressed
more and more. The Dean of the Evening College is responsible to the President of the University.

VII. Student Recruitment

Newspaper publicity (especially during the summer and
before major registration periods) is widely used. Special
motivational appeals have been developed for industry, especially with training directors, and professional organizations.

* * *

University of Kentucky
Evening Class Program
Total enrollment 26,450   Public Institution
Evening enrollment 1,435   Semester System

I. Admission Policies

Deadline for application for admission is one month
prior to registration. Students may register for credit
courses before transcripts are submitted. Non-degree students may register for credit classes. Non-degree students
must be eligible for credit at time of enrollment in order to
meet admission requirements. Evening students must maintain a 2.0 grade point average. There is no special degree
program for adults and none considered. Admission Policies are set by the Dean of Admissions. Day and evening
students may enroll in the same classes if space is available.

II.   Terminology

Title of Division: Evening Class Program, defined: non-degree students meeting classes after 5 p. m.   Continuing Education: includes credit and non-credit classes offered under same conditions as similar daytime campus classes.

III.   Fees

Day students pay $12. 50 per credit hour; evening students pay $14 per credit hour.   This is justified because the evening classes are financially self-supporting.

IV.   Faculty and Faculty Recruitment

85% teaching evening classes are full-time.   Final authority to hire faculty members lies with the Academic Chairman.   Regular faculty meetings are not held for the evening faculty.

V.   Scheduling

The Director of the Evening Class Program is responsible for the evening class schedule.   The Director has the authority to revise the evening class schedule.   Three credit hour classes are scheduled two nights a week.   Part-time evening students are not eligible for the Dean's List.

VI.   General

In general, all evening divisions are not receiving adequate support.   The Director of the Evening Class Program is responsible to the Dean of University Extension.

VII.   Student Recruitment

Newspaper, radio and television publicity are used.

* * *

LaSalle College
Evening Division
Philadelphia, Pa.

Total enrollment 6, 368   Church-related Institution
Evening enrollment 3, 148   Semester System

I. Admission Policies

Deadline for application for admission is eight days before classes begin. Students may not register for credit courses without transcripts. Non-degree students may take a maximum of eight hours of credit work and must already have a bachelor's degree. Students must maintain 1. 00 after 33 semester hours; 1. 50 after 66 hours; 1. 75 after 99 hours. There is no special degree program for adults and none considered. Admission policies are set by the Evening Division Committee. Day and evening students may enroll in the same classes when courses correspond. Orientation for evening students is held before registration.

II. Terminology

Title of Division: LaSalle College Evening Division, defined: regular collegiate degree-oriented programs offered in the evening.

III. Fees

Day school students pay an annual fee of $1400; evening students pay $30 per credit hour. Refunds of 90% are made in the first week of classes; 80% in the second week; 70% in the third; 60% in the fourth; 50% in the fifth; 40% in the sixth; 30% in the seventh; none thereafter.

IV. Faculty and Faculty Recruitment

33% teaching evening classes are full time. The final authority to hire evening faculty lies with the Dean of the Evening Division. Some full-time faculty members teach exclusively in the evening and are responsible to the Dean of the Evening Division. Regular faculty meetings are held.

V. Scheduling

The Dean of the Evening Division is responsible for the evening class schedule in cooperation with the Assistant Dean. Three credit hour classes are scheduled two nights a week. Part-time evening students are eligible for the Dean's List after completing 33 hours with a minimum of 3. 40.

VI. General

Students participate in discussion concerning academic programs through the Academic Affairs Committee and Student Congress. The Evening Division is receiving adequate support. The Dean of the Evening Division is responsible to the Academic Vice President. Audio-visual instructional aids are available for evening classes.

VII. Student Recruitment

Newspaper and radio publicity are used. Special motivational appeals have been developed for industry.

* * *

Louisiana State University
University College
Baton Rouge, Louisiana

Total enrollment 18, 253   Public Institution
University College enrollment   Semester System
   1, 096

I. Admission Policies

Application for admission to evening classes must be submitted prior to registration. Non-matriculating students may register for credit courses without transcripts if a statement of good standing is provided from the last college or university attended. There is no maximum number of hours that a non-degree student may take. A student may register for a maximum of 12 hours per semester and 10 hours per summer session. A requirement for admission for regular students is a transcript from all colleges attended; if no prior college work, a high school transcript is necessary. To be in good standing a "C" average must be maintained by the students. The Bachelor of Science in General Studies degree is offered. Enrollment is 1, 096. Admission policies are set by the Board of Supervisors of the Univer-

Louisiana State University (cont.)

sity. Day and evening students may enroll in the same classes.

II. Terminology

Title of Division: University College, which is a senior college of the University. Continuing Education is any type of education for students or individuals enrolled in credit or non-credit courses for vocational or avocational purposes.

III. Fees

There is no fee differential between day and evening classes. Refunds of 90% are made before classes begin; 75% during first two weeks; 50% during third and fourth week; none thereafter.

IV. Faculty and Faculty Recruitment

Final authority for hiring evening faculty lies with the Dean of each respective college and the Office of Academic Affairs. No full-time faculty members teach exclusively in the evenings.

V. Scheduling

Department Chairmen are responsible for the Evening class schedule. Three credit hour classes are scheduled one and two nights a week.

VI. General

Evening Division is not receiving adequate support. The Dean of University College is responsible to the Dean of Academic Affairs.

VII. Student Recruitment

Special motivational appeals have been developed for industry.

130

Louisiana State University in New Orleans
New Orleans, Louisiana
Evening Division

Total enrollment 9,000   Public Institution
Evening enrollment 1,200   Semester System

I. Admission Policies

There is no deadline for application for admission to
evening classes. Students may register for credit courses
before transcripts are submitted. Admission requirements
for all students include a transcript from each institution
previously attended. Graduates of state approved high schools
are admitted on basis of high school diploma; graduates of
out of state high schools are admitted on basis of achievement and aptitude. The ACT scores are used for placement
in English and Mathematics. No mail registration is used.
The Board of Supervisors of the University formulate the admission policies. Day and evening students may enroll in
the same class. An Orientation Program for evening students is held just prior to registration.

II. Terminology

Title of Division: Evening Division, defined: "The administrative unit which keeps the academic records of students taking classes at night." Continuing Education, defined:
"Continuing Education is a life-long project--either for credit
or non-credit, either formally or informally."

III. Fees

There is no fee differential between day and evening
classes. A refund for reduction of hours carried is made if
the drop occurs before the date specified to add courses for
credit. Refunds of 90% are made for resignations before
classes begin, 75% during the first two weeks, 50% during
the third and fourth weeks, and none thereafter.

IV. Faculty and Faculty Recruitment

All evening classes are taught by the regular faculty.
The Dean of each college hires his own faculty. No full-time

Louisiana State Univ. -New Orleans (cont.)

faculty members teach exclusively in the evening. No regular faculty meetings are held for the evening faculty. The
Dean of each senior college is responsible for any overloads
taught by his own faculty.

V. Scheduling

The department chairmen submit a schedule for evening classes to the Dean of Academic Affairs for approval.
The Director of the Evening Division may suggest classes to
be offered in the evening. Thred credit-hour classes are scheduled two nights a week. There is no difference in quality between day and evening classes. Part-time evening students
are not eligible for the Dean's List.

VI. General

Students do not participate in any discussion regarding the academic program. In general, the evening division
could use more support in terms of additional programs and
financing. The Director of the Evening Division is responsible to the Dean of Academic Affairs.

VII. Student Recruitment

Newspaper articles are used for publicity, but no advertising is permitted. Public service announcements are
prepared for radio and television.

* * *

University of Louisville
Louisville, Kentucky
University College

Total enrollment 10, 000   Private Institution
Evening enrollment 2, 300   Semester System

I. Admission Policies

There is no deadline for application for admission to
evening classes. Non-degree students may register for credit courses without transcripts and may take a maximum of

twelve hours.   Regular students must have been in the upper
half of their high school graduating class.   Students are
placed on probation with a 6-12 quality point deficiency and
dismissed with a 13 point deficiency.   There is no special
degree program for adults.   Admission policies are set by
the faculty.   Day and evening students may register in the
same classes.   Orientation for evening students is held during the fall and spring.

II.   Terminology

Title of Division: University College, defined: Encompasses all Continuing Education Programs.

III.   Fees

Evening students do not pay the student activity fees
that day students pay.   Refunds are made on a graduating
percentage basis.

IV.   Faculty and Faculty Recruitment

40% teaching evening classes are full time.   Final authority to hire evening faculty lies with the Dean of University College, and he may reject a faculty member assigned
to teach evening classes or engage an instructor without the
consent of department chairmen.   Regular faculty meetings
are held every fall.   Each full-time faculty member may
teach one course per semester on an overload basis and may
participate in non-credit courses as needed.

V.   Scheduling

The Dean of University College is responsible for the
evening class schedule, and has the authority to revise and
make additions to it.   Three credit hour courses are scheduled both one and two nights a week.   Part-time evening students are eligible for the Dean's List with a "B" average after completing 7 hours.

VI.   General

The evening division is receiving adequate support.

University of Louisville (cont.)

The Dean of University College is responsible to the President of the University. Audio-visual instructional aids are available for use in evening classes.

VII. Student Recruitment

Newspaper and radio publicity are used.

* * *

Loyola University
Evening College
Baltimore, Maryland

Total enrollment 850 (day)   Church-related Institution
Evening enrollment 1,340;   Semester System
  700 (graduate)

I. Admission Policies

There is no deadline for application for admission to evening classes. Students may register without transcripts provisionally. Non-degree students may take an equivalent of two full academic years of work. Admission requirements are high school graduation or college transcript. Mail registration is used: Course selection forms and schedules are mailed to all students; they are filled out and mailed to the college. The Dean and Assistant Dean approve them. Class cards are mailed to the student; they are filled out and returned to the college with tuition fees. Students must maintain a 2.0 average. There is no special degree program for adults. Admission policies are set by the Dean of the Evening College with approval of the President and Board of Trustees. Day and evening students may enroll in the same classes with deans' approval. Orientation is conducted by the Evening Student Council during the first week of classes. All students are on a probationary status until successful completion of sixteen semester hours.

II. Terminology

Title of Division: Loyola Evening College, defined: Programs similar to day, but offered in evening hours usually to fully employed, older students.

134

III. Fees

Day students pay $1,100 annually; evening students pay $30 per semester hour. Refunds are made during the first two weeks of 80%; 60%, second two weeks; 40%, third two weeks; 20%, fourth two weeks.

IV. Faculty and Faculty Recruitment

20% teaching evening classes are full-time. Final authority to hire evening faculty lies with the Academic Vice-President in cooperation with the Dean and Department Chairmen. Some full-time faculty members teach exclusively in the evening. Regular faculty meetings for each department are held each semester. One overload course is permitted each semester for faculty members.

V. Scheduling

The Dean of the Evening College is responsible for the evening class schedule. Three credit hour classes are scheduled two nights a week. Part-time evening students are eligible for the Dean's List after completing nine semester hours with a "B" or better in all courses.

VI. General

Some informal tutorial work is being done in economically deprived off-campus locations. Students participate in discussions regarding the academic program through the student council and membership in the curriculum committee. The evening division is receiving adequate support. The Dean of the Evening College is responsible to the Academic Vice-President. Audio-visual instructional aids are available for evening classes.

VII. Student Recruitment

Newspaper, radio and television publicity are used. Special motivational appeals have been developed for industry and civic organizations such as the Chamber of Commerce.

* * *

135

Loyola University
University College
Chicago, Illinois

Total enrollment 13,548   Church-related Institution
Evening enrollment 2,565   Semester System

I.   Admission Policies

Deadline for application for admission for evening students is registration day.   Students may register for credit
courses without transcripts.   Admission requirements are
high school graduation or equivalent or in good standing at
college previously attended.   There is no limit to the amount
of work taken as a non-matriculating student, only that he
remains in good academic standing.   Mail registration is
used.   Students must maintain a 2.0.   There is no special
degree program for adults.   Admission policies are set by
the Committee on Admissions.   Day and evening students may
enroll in the same classes with permission.

II.   Terminology

Title of Division: University College, defined: The
part-time, degree-granting division which offers classes in
the late afternoon, evening and on Saturday.

III.   Fees

Day students are charged $50 per semester hour;
evening students: $35.   Refunds are based on a graduating
percentage basis.

IV.   Faculty and Faculty Recruitment

50% teaching evening classes are full time.   Final authority to hire evening faculty lies with the Committee on
Faculty appointments.   The Dean of University College can
reject a faculty member assigned to teach evening classes,
and may engage an instructor without the consent of a department chairman.   Overloads for faculty members are not
permitted.

The Dean of University College is responsible for the evening class schedule, and has the authority to revise it. Three credit hour classes are scheduled both one and two nights per week. Part-time evening students are eligible for the Dean's List with a 3.20 or better after completing 20 semester hours.

VI. General

The evening division is receiving adequate support. The Dean of University College is responsible to the Academic Vice-President.

VII. Student Recruitment

Newspaper and radio publicity are used.

* * *

Loyola University
Evening Division
New Orleans, La.

Total enrollment 4,500   Church-related Institution
Evening enrollment 1,300   Semester System

I. Admission Policies

There is no deadline for application for admission and students may register without transcripts. Admission requirements are high school diploma, examination or advanced standing. The Bachelor of Arts and Bachelor of Commercial Science Degrees are offered for adults in the evening, these degrees differ in requirements from the day degree and are awarded by the Evening Division. Admission policies are set by the University Committee on Admission Policies and Standards. Day and evening students may enroll in the same classes only with permission of the Director of the Evening Division. Orientation for evening students is held the day before the opening of each semester.

II. Terminology

Title of Division: Evening Division which like other

137

Loyola Univ. - New Orleans (cont.)

schools and colleges is answerable to the Academic Vice-President. Continuing education is credit or non-credit (creditable courses not now being applied to a degree) courses scheduled by adults.

III. Fees

Part-time day students pay $50 per semester hour; evening students pay $22 per semester hour. Refunds of 80% are made during the first week; 60% during the second and third weeks; 40% during the third to fifth week and none thereafter.

IV. Faculty and Faculty Recruitment

Ten faculty members teaching evening classes are from the day faculty. Five full-time faculty members teach exclusively in the evening. Regular faculty meetings are held each semester. Faculty members are paid $500 for three semester courses taught on an overload basis.

V. Scheduling

The Dean of the Evening Division is responsible for the evening class schedule and has the authority to revise or make additions in it. Three credit hour classes are scheduled both one and two nights a week. Part-time evening students are eligible for the Dean's List after completing 9 semester hours with a 3.0.

VI. General

Candidates for graduation make suggestions for future schedules. The Evening Division is receiving adequate support. The Dean of the Evening Division is responsible to the Academic Vice President. Audio-visual instructional aids are available for evening classes.

VII. Student Recruitment

Newspaper, radio and television publicity are used.
* * *
138

Total enrollment 3,500   Private Institution
Evening enrollment 469   Semester System

I.   Admission Policies

Deadline for application for admission for evening students is a month prior to registration.   Students may register for credit courses without transcripts if they are submitted within a reasonable time.   Non-degree students may take
a maximum of 33 semester hours work.   Admission requirement for non-matriculating students is high school graduation;
for regular students, high school graduation, college board
scores and recommendations.   Mail registration is not used.
A grade point average of 2.0 must be maintained over every
period of 33 credits; a 2.0 is required for graduation on a
4.0 scale.   CEEB Tests are required if applicant is within
four years of separation from high school.   A special degree
for adults, Associate in Applied Science, is offered; a Bachelor's degree in this field is being considered.   Admission
policies are set by the Admissions Office.   Day and evening
students may enroll in the same classes with permission.
There is no orientation program for evening students.

II.   Terminology

Title of Division: Evening Division, defined: The
Evening Division is an integral unit of the College, its primary purpose is identical with the objectives of the College
as described in the college catalog.   It is a separate academic unit under its own director and awards the Baccalaureate degree and Associate in Applied Science degree.

III.   Fees

Day students pay a yearly blanket charge; evening
students pay per credit.   Refunds are made on a graduating
percentage basis.

IV.   Faculty and Faculty Recruitment

53% teaching evening classes are full time.   Final

Manhattan College (cont.)

authority to hire evening faculty lies with the Director in consultation with the Department Chairmen and the Academic Vice-President. The Director can engage an instructor without the consent of department chairmen, and full-time evening faculty are responsible to him. Regular faculty meetings are held once a semester. Faculty members are not permitted to teach over the maximum of 12 hours per semester.

V. Scheduling

The Director of the Evening Division is responsible for the evening class schedule, and he has the authority to revise it. Three credit hour courses are scheduled two nights per week. Part-time evening students are eligible for the Dean's List with a 3.0 or above after completing eight credits or more.

VI. General

Students participate in discussions regarding the academic program through the Faculty Relations Committee made up of full- and part-time students. The evening division is receiving adequate support. The Director of the Evening Division is responsible to the Academic Vice-President. Audio-visual instructional aids are available for evening classes.

VII. Student Recruitment

Newspaper and radio publicity are used. Special motivational appeals have been developed for Industry and Civic Organizations.

* * *

Marquette University
Liberal Arts Evening Division
Total enrollment 12,264   Church-related Institution
Evening enrollment 722   Semester System

I. Admission Policies

Deadline for application for admission is one month

prior to registration. Students may register for credit courses without transcripts. Non-degree students may take an unlimited amount of courses for credit. Admission requirements are high school graduation or equivalent and at least 21 years of age. A special degree for adults is offered: Associate in Arts in Law Enforcement, enrollment: 51. Day and evening students may enroll in the same classes.

II. Terminology

Title of Division: Liberal Arts Evening Division, defined: a semi-autonomous division of the day school.

III. Fees

Evening students pay proportionately less per credit in order to meet competition with public institutions. Refunds are made on a sliding scale basis whereby 10% of the charges are refunded for each week up to the 10th week of classes.

IV. Faculty and Faculty Recruitment

80% teaching evening classes are full-time. Final authority to hire evening faculty lies with Department Chairmen and Dean of the College. Full-time faculty members are not permitted to teach on an overload basis except in some cases. No full-time faculty members teach exclusively in the evening.

V. Scheduling

The Director of the Liberal Arts Evening Division is responsible for the evening class schedule only on a consultative basis. Department Chairmen and the Dean of the College are responsible. Three credit hour classes are scheduled two nights a week. Research is underway which will explore the desirability and feasibility of offering unique adult degree programs at Marquette University. Part-time evening students are not eligible for the Dean's List but, it is under consideration.

VI. General

Students participate in discussion regarding academic

141

Marquette University (cont.)

programs on a very limited basis. In general, all evening divisions are not receiving adequate support. The Director of the Liberal Arts Evening Division is responsible to the Dean of the College of Liberal Arts. Audio-visual instructional aids are available for evening classes.

* * *

University of Maryland
University College
College Park, Maryland

Total enrollment 32,000   Public Institution
Evening enrollment 10,543,   Semester System
   (State of Maryland only.)

I. Admission Policies

Deadline for application for admission is prior to registration for non-adults; adults may register for credit courses pending receipt of transcripts, and may take an unlimited amount of hours as special students. Admission requirements for adults are graduation from an approved high school and good standing at college previously attended; non-adults: graduation from approved high school and "C" average in previous college work. GED with specified scores, may be substituted for diploma. No mail registration is used. A student is dismissed after completing 12-20 hours below a .35; 21-35 hours below 1.35; 36-50 hours below 1.65; 51-65 hours below 1.80; 66-80 hours below 1.90; 81+ hours below a 1.95. A special degree program for adults is offered: Bachelor of Arts (General Studies curriculum; Enrollment: 5,000). A special degree program is being considered at graduate level: M.S. in Social Science, M.A. in Liberal Studies; at undergraduate level B.A. (Political Science concentration). Admission policies are set by the Dean, Directors and general administration. Day students may enroll in evening classes with permission of their dean.

II. Terminology

Title of Division: University College (Three credit division operating in Maryland and three credit divisions overseas, plus a conference and institute division and a residential center of adult education,) defined: A service-oriented administrative unit facilitating the continuing education

142

responsibilities of the University and which also grants degrees.

III. Fees

Graduate students pay higher tuition than part-time day or evening students. Refunds vary as to the type of action and date of action.

IV. Faculty and Faculty Recruitment

40 to 45% teaching evening classes are full-time. Final authority to hire faculty lies with department chairmen. Some full-time faculty members teach exclusively in the evening. They are responsible to the Dean of University College, administratively and to the department chairmen, academically. Faculty members are limited to an overload of an equivalent of six semester hours in an academic year, (fall and spring semester).

V. Scheduling

The Dean of University College is responsible for the schedule. Directors coordinate courses, then a consolidated list is sent to departments with requests to staff; 3 credit hour classes are scheduled either 1 or two nights a week. Part-time students are eligible for the Dean's List after completing 15 semester hours with a 3.5 average.

VI. General

Special eight week terms are offered at military centers. In general, evening divisions are not receiving adequate support. The Dean is responsible to the President and Vice-President (Academic and Administrative). Audio-visual instructional aids are used.

VII. Student Recruitment

Newspaper publicity--three advertisements per year are used.

* * *

McNeese State College
Evening School

Total enrollment 5,090   State Institution
Evening enrollment 380   Semester System

I. Admission Policies

Deadline for application for admission is registration day. Students may register provisionally without transcripts. Admission requirements are high school graduation or GED and maturity. Students must maintain a passing average and attend all classes. A special degree for adults is being considered. Admission policies are set by the Dean's Council and the Registrar's Office. All day school regulations apply to evening students without exceptions.

II. Terminology

Title of Division: Evening School (it ranks above a department but below a division; the coordinator is considered a department head.)

III. Fees

There is no fee differential between day and evening classes. Refunds are made to students on a graduating percentage basis.

IV. Faculty and Faculty Recruitment

100% teaching evening classes are full time. Final authority to hire evening faculty lies with Department Chairmen. Regular faculty meetings are held once a semester. If faculty members teach courses on an overload basis, they receive extra compensation.

V. Scheduling

The Coordinator of the Evening School is responsible for the evening class schedule. Three credit hour classes are scheduled one night a week. Part-time evening students are not eligible for the Dean's List.

VI. General

Extension courses are taught at Fort Polk, Louisiana. In general, all evening divisions are receiving adequate support. The Coordinator of Evening School is responsible to the Dean of Humanities. Audio-visual instructional aids are available as needed.

VII. Student Recruitment

Newspaper (twice a semester) and radio (once a year, interview) publicity are used. Special motivational appeals have been developed for industry and civic organizations.

* * *

Memphis State University
Division of Continuing Studies
Total enrollment 16, 330   Public Institution
Evening enrollment 5, 000+   Semester System

I. Admission Policies

There is no deadline for application for admission to evening classes. Students may register for credit courses before transcripts are received and take a maximum of 18 semester hours as non-matriculating students. Admission requirements for special students is high school graduation or at least 21 years of age; for regular students, acceptable ACT scores, high school transcript, health card, etc. Students having attempted at least 12 hours must maintain a quality point total of 18 less than twice the number of cumulative hours attempted based on a 4.0 scale. A special degree program for adults is being considered. Admission policies are set by State Board of Education. Day and evening students may enroll in the same classes; approximately one-half of the evening students take some day courses. Orientation for evening students is held prior to registration.

II. Terminology

Title of Division: Division of Continuing Studies, defined: Division offering functions to service needs of students who do not choose to make college work a full-time objective.

III. Fees

Refunds are made on a graduating percentage basis of 80% to 0% declining weekly from first day of class.

IV. Faculty and Faculty Recruitment

Approximately 75% teaching evening classes are full time. The final authority to hire evening faculty lies with Department Chairmen and College Deans. Regular faculty meetings are held with department chairmen and Deans. Faculty members may teach one course per academic year on an overload basis.

V. Scheduling

The Director of the Division of Continuing Studies is partially responsible for the evening schedule. Schedules are submitted to the Registrar by the department chairmen. Three credit hour classes are scheduled both one and two nights a week. Day and evening classes are equal in all respects in terms of quality. Part-time evening students are eligible for the Dean's List with a 3.4 after completing 15 semester hours.

VI. General

Some off-campus special courses are being offered for economically deprived populations. Students participate very little in discussions regarding the academic program. The evening division is receiving adequate financial support but, in general, all evening divisions do not receive adequate professional support. The Director of the Division of Continuing Studies is responsible to the University Provost. Audio-visual instructional aids are available for evening classes.

VII. Student Recruitment

Newspaper publicity is used in addition to mail distribution of university literature to business, industry, public libraries, etc. * * *

Miami-Dade Junior College
Special Programs Division
Total enrollment 8, 100   Public Institution
Evening and Weekend College
    enrollment: 3, 686 Individuals;
    5, 786 section registrations

I. Admission Policies

There is no deadline for application for admission; a student may register for credit courses without transcripts. A limit of 12 hours may be taken as a non-matriculating student. Admission requirement for special students: 19 years of age or older; regular students: high school graduation or GED. All students are dismissed after completion of 72 hours without acquiring a 1. 5; special students must attain a "C" average in initial 12 hours. A special degree program is not offered and is under consideration. Admission policies are set by the President's Council. There are no restrictions on day and evening students enrolling in the same class.

II. Terminology

Title of Division: Division of Special Programs, defined: Any education program scheduled evenings, weekends and off-campus for persons beyond what was formerly regarded as "normal" school age.

III. Fees

Refund policies: 100% first five days of class; 50% after fifth but before end of the 10th day; none thereafter.

IV. Faculty and Faculty Recruitment

90% teaching evening classes are full-time. Final authority to hire evening faculty lies with department chairmen. Faculty may not teach overload except with consent of the academic dean.

V. Scheduling

The Dean of Special Programs must approve the

schedule but the department chairmen are responsible for it. The Director of Special Programs may make changes in the schedule. Three credit hour classes are scheduled either one or two nights a week.

VI. General

Special Programs Division is receiving adequate support. The Director of the Special Programs Division is responsible to the Academic Dean. Complete audio-visual services are available to all instructors.

VII. Student Recruitment

Newspaper, radio and television (Junior College Forum) publicity are used.

* * *

Millard Fillmore College
State University of New York
Buffalo, N. Y.

Total enrollment 20,000   Public Institution
Evening enrollment 6,000   Semester System

I. Admission Policies

Deadline for application for admission for fall semester is July 18; for spring semester December 1. There is no limit on the number of hours that may be taken as a "special" student. Students may register without transcripts only in individual cases where such transcripts are not available through no fault of the student. The admission requirement for "special" students is high school graduation or GED. For regular day students a high school academic average of 80 is required. No ACT or CEEB scores are required for admission. The college is considering offering a special degree program for adults to be offered at a later date. No mail registration is used. The Dean and his staff formulate the admission policies for evening students with the permission of the faculty senate. Evening students receive priority for enrollment in evening classes--day students may enroll as space permits. An Orientation Program is held for evening students two weeks before the official registration for the fall semester.

II. Terminology

Title of Division: Division of Continuing Education, Defined: "Educational opportunities offered by the University beyond those offered in articulated day school programs." Continuing Education defined: "All educational opportunities beyond articulated daytime (full time student) programs."

III. Fees

The same fees are paid by part time and full time students--day or evening. Student activity fees do differ, i. e., compulsory athletic fee is paid by day students. A graduated refund policy is used.

IV. Faculty and Faculty Recruitment

Approximately 50% of the evening faculty are full-time. The Dean of Continuing Education is responsible for the evening class schedule. Members of the Dean's staff organize the semester by semester schedule of classes in face-to-face meetings with day deans and departmental chairmen. The Evening College staff organizes the desired classes and works out problems of approval, staffing, budget, etc. Three-credit-hour classes are scheduled on either one or two nights per week depending on the nature of the subject. Day and evening classes compare favorably in quality but traditional feeling persists of lower quality of evening classes on the part of day faculty. Part-time evening students are eligible for the Dean's List. Students must take 6 or more semester hours with a minimal 2.0 average (based on the 4.0 system).

VI. General

Students participate extensively in discussions regarding the academic program. The institution offers tutorial programs for the disadvantaged--some admission requirements are waived for this group of students. In general, the administration recognizes the need and importance of the adult education program, but adequate stress and financial support has not been realized. The Dean of Continuing Education is directly responsible to the President.

Millard Fillmore College (cont.)

VII. Student Recruitment

All forms of publicity are used--newspaper articles and advertisements, radio and television. Special appeals and publicity material are prepared for industry and civic clubs and organizations in the city.

* * *

Milliken University
Adult Education and Evening School
Total enrollment 1,400   Public Institution
Evening enrollment 600   Semester System

I. Admission Policies

Deadline for application for admission to evening classes is one week prior to registration. Applications taken after that time are placed on temporary registration status. Students may register under temporary registration without transcripts. Non-matriculating students may take a maximum of eight semester hours. Admission requirements are upper 3/4 of high school graduating class or admitted on probation, and satisfactory scores on tests. There is no special degree program for adults. Admission policies are set by the Dean's Council, administration and faculty. Very few day and evening students enroll in the same classes.

II. Terminology

Title of Division: Adult Education and Evening School, defined: Division offering credit and/or non-credit courses as well as conferences, seminars, short courses, etc.

III. Fees

Day students pay $56 per semester hour; evening students pay $42 per semester hour. Refunds of 90% are made if withdrawal is during the first week of class; 50% during first month; none after one month elapses.

IV. Faculty and Faculty Recruitment

Approximately 50% teaching evening classes are full-

time.   Final authority to hire evening faculty members lies
with the Director of Adult Education and the Evening School
in cooperation with department chairmen.   The Director may
reject a faculty member assigned to teach evening classes.
Regular faculty meetings are not held.   Faculty members
teaching courses on an overload basis are paid according to
rank and receive the same rate for credit or non-credit
courses.

V.   Scheduling

The Director of the Adult Education and Evening
School is responsible for the evening class schedule and has
the authority to revise it.   Three credit hour classes are
held one night a week.   Part-time evening students are not
eligible for the Dean's List.

VI.   General

Students participate in discussions regarding academic
programs through counseling sessions.   The evening division
is receiving adequate support.   The Director of the Adult
Education and Evening School is responsible to the Dean of
the University.   Audio-visual instructional aids are available
for evening classes.

VII.   Student Recruitment

Newspaper, radio and television publicity are used.
Special motivational appeals have been developed for industry
and Chambers of Commerce.

* * *

University of Minnesota
Department of Evening and Special Classes

Total enrollment 41,000   Public Institution
Evening enrollment 27,000   Simultaneous Quarter,
                                                    Semester, and Semes-
                                                    ter Schedule
                                                    (Quarter Credits)

I.   Admission Policies

Since there are no admission requirements for evening

151

University of Minnesota (cont.)

and special classes, there is no deadline for application for admission. Students may register for credit courses without transcripts. Non-matriculated students may take an unlimited amount of work for credit. Mail registration is used: student requests registration material, fills out forms and submits them with his tuition fees. No special degree program for adults. Evening students register in day classes primarily in Music and Library courses; day students may register in any evening classes.

II. Terminology

Title of Division: Department of Evening and Special Classes, General Extension Division.

III. Fees

Evening class tuition is $13 per credit hour; day class tuition reaches its maximum at 12 credits. Refunds are made on a graduated percentage basis.

IV. Faculty and Faculty Recruitment

80% teaching evening classes are full-time day school teachers. Final authority to hire evening faculty lies with the Director of Evening and Special Classes. The Director may reject a faculty member assigned to each evening classes. A few faculty members teach exclusively in the evening. Some evening class faculty teach evening classes as part of their regular "day" load. No regular faculty meetings are held.

V. Scheduling

The Director of Evening and Special Classes is responsible for the evening class schedule. The Director has the authority to revise the evening class schedule, completed in cooperation with academic departments. Most three-credit-hour courses are scheduled one night a week. Day and evening classes are similar. Part-time evening students are not eligible for the Dean's List.

VI. General

Some special programs are offered in neighborhood locations for economically deprived populations. Students participate very little in discussions regarding academic programs. The Director of the Department of Evening and Special Classes is responsible to the Associate Dean of the Division. Audio-visual instructional aids are available for use in evening classes.

VII. Student Recruitment

In addition to the distribution of 75,000 Evening and Special Class bulletins, newspaper, radio, television and direct mail publicity are used.

* * *

Nassau Community College
Garden City, N.Y.
Evening Division

Total enrollment 13,154   Public Institution
Evening enrollment 7,250   Semester System

I. Admission Policies

Deadline for application for admission for fall semester is June 1 for regular students and September-October for non-matriculating students. Students may take up to 18 hours as "special" students. Admission requirements include a high school diploma or equivalency for "special" students and a 82 high school average and 450/450 board scores for regular students. No CEEB is required for adults, but placement tests in Reading and English are required. No mail registration is used. Retention policies are "open" --with advisement and counseling used to determine continuation of enrollment. The Dean of Instruction formulates the admission policies. Day and evening students may enroll in the same class by special permission. An Orientation Program for evening students is scheduled.

II. Terminology

Title of Division: Evening Division, defined: The Evening Division is the administrative unit of the college which initiates, guides, facilitates and provides leadership

Nassau Community College (cont.)

in a many faceted program for those persons not regularly
enrolled as day students on the campus.

III. Fees

There is no differential in fees between day and evening classes. Applications for refunds are referred to a
committee. If withdrawal is beyond the control of the student, the fee is refunded.

IV.   Faculty and Faculty Recruitment

There is no policy regarding the percentage of faculty
for evening classes that are full-time faculty members. At
the present time 30% of the evening faculty are full-time.
The Dean of Instruction has the authority for hiring full- and
part-time faculty members. There are no full-time faculty
members who teach exclusively in the evening. Regular faculty meetings are held for evening faculty in September, February, and June. Faculty members may teach on overload--
limited to 18 credit hours over an academic year.

V. Scheduling

The Dean of Instruction is responsible for the evening
class schedule. Three-hour classes are scheduled on two
nights per week. A research project has been completed on
the "Cooperative Opportunity in Public Education (COPE)."
Day and evening classes compare favorably in quality. Evening students are eligible for the Dean's List. 12 hours
must be taken during the year with a 3.00 GPA.

VI.   General

Limited opportunity is given students to participate in
discussions regarding the academic program, but students do
serve on the Curriculum Committee. Adequate support is
given to the evening program by the administration. The
Dean is responsible directly to the President of the College.

Newspaper articles and advertisements are used for publicity purposes as well as radio.

* * *

New Haven College
West Haven, Conn.
Division of Continuing Education
Total enrollment 4,000   Private Institution
Evening enrollment 1,900   Semester System

I. Admission Policies

Deadline for application for admission for fall semester is September 5. Students may register provisionally providing some proof of academic ability is available. Students may take 30 sem. hrs. in courses other than English or Mathematics as "special" students. CEEB scores are accepted but the New Haven College Placement tests are required for admission in addition to high school transcripts. Students must maintain a QPR of 1.5 each semester. Less than 1.00 means dismissal. Mail registration is used and all students are sent a pre-registration packet approximately one month prior to the registration period. New Haven College is considering offering a special degree program for adults--possibly for adult women. Admission policies are formulated by the Admissions and Standing Committee of the college. Day and evening students may enroll in the same class with permission from the scheduling department. No orientation program is scheduled for evening students.

II. Terminology

Title of Division: Division of Continuing Education, defined: Evening, Summer School and Extension Classes-- Also Division of Special Studies.

III. Fees

Cost for day students - $10 application fee, $25 acceptance fee and $500 tuition. Evening fees include $10 application fee and $30 per semester hour credit. Refunds are pro-rated the first four weeks of school--after that no refund is given.

New Haven College (cont.)

IV. Faculty and Faculty Recruitment

There is no policy regarding the percentage of full-time faculty members that are required for evening classes. At the present time, 20% of the evening faculty are full-time. The authority to hire faculty lies with department chairmen. There are no full-time faculty members hired exclusively for the evening program. Regular faculty meetings are held for evening faculty during Orientation before each semester. All full time faculty are allowed to carry one 3 semester hour course overload in their schedule.

V. Scheduling

The Director is responsible for scheduling. Three-hour classes are scheduled one night per week, due to the normal commuting problem. Day and evening classes are identical in quality. Part-time students are eligible for the Dean's List with the accumulation of a minimum of 14 semester hours with a GPA of 3.20.

VI. General

Students do participate in discussion regarding the academic program. Many changes and additions are requested by students and then referred to either the Faculty Senate or individual chairmen. In general, the Division of Continuing Education is receiving adequate stress and support from the administration. The Director is responsible to the Vice President and the President of the College.

VII. Student Recruitment

Newspaper articles and advertisements are used for publicity purposes. Special motivational appeals are developed for industry as well as for various organizations such as the Chamber of Commerce.

* * *

The New School
New York, N. Y.
A Division for Social Research
Total enrollment 12, 697   Private Institution
Evening enrollment 2, 700   Semester System

I. Admission Policies

Deadline for application for admission is two weeks
after classes begin (credit students) and three weeks after
classes begin for students enrolling for non-credit.   Students
may register before transcripts are submitted.   Non-degree
or "special" students may take a maximum of 12 semester
hours before matriculating as degree students.   Admission
requirements include high school graduation--no ACT or CEEB
is required.   No special adult degree program is offered.
All evening courses are open to day students, but day classes
are not open to adults.   No Orientation Program is scheduled
for evening students.

II. Terminology

A Division of the New School for Social Research defined.   "covers all non-degree courses--includes certificate
programs (day and evening). "

III. Fees

There is a fee differential between day and evening
classes.   A yearly tuition is charged to day students--un-
limited courses.   The evening tuition is per course and by
credit.   The institution gives a proportional refund depending
on date of withdrawal up to the 3rd week of classes.

IV. Faculty and Faculty Recruitment

There are no full-time faculty teaching evening classes.
The authority to hire faculty lies with the Dean.   No regular
faculty meetings are held for evening faculty.   No overloads
are permitted.

V.   Scheduling

The Dean is responsible for scheduling.   Evening
classes are submitted by the faculty but the schedule is
mediated by necessity of space allocation.   Three-hour
classes are scheduled one night per week.   According to the
Dean, day and evening classes are totally different and therefore incomparable.   The day courses are of generally higher
quality.   Evening students are not eligible for the Dean's
List.

VI.   General

Day students participate in discussions regarding the
academic program, but evening students are not involved with
these discussions.   The day program is conducted totally by
examination--there are no credits and no grades given.   In
general, adequate support is given to the evening program.
The Dean is directly responsible to the President of the
School.

VII.   Student Recruitment

Newspaper articles and advertisements are used for
publicity purposes.   Special motivational appeals are developed for industry as well as for various civic organizations.

* * *

New York University
Private Institution

Note: The material submitted from New York University
pertains solely to the School of Continuing Education
and Extension Services which is largely devoted to
non-credit courses, lecture series, workshops, conferences, and institutes; these last year accounted for
33,795 registrations of a total of 36,031 registrations.
The remaining 2,236 registrations were in four special degree programs.

I.   Admission Policies

Applications are ordinarily received before June 1,
for the fall semester; no student is admitted without application, transcripts and relevant test scores.   There are no

non-degree or special students with credit. Admission requirements for the different degree programs vary according to the special case. * They are Associate in Arts (evening degree program for adults), Associate in Applied Science (Business) for adults; Associate in Applied Science in Early Childhood Education and Social Work (daytime program with sections for adults and sections for recent high school graduates); New York University Opportunities Program (for those with grades ordinarily less than 10% of ordinary admission requirements). There is no mail registration for credit courses. Special Degrees enrollment: 181-Associate in Arts (evening); 132-Associate in Applied Science (Business-evening); 60-Associate in Applied Science (Early Childhood Education and Social Work--daytime). The fourth special degree program involves 53 students with the majority attending on Martin Luther King, Jr., scholarships. Admission policies are set by the faculty of the school. Part-time students may enroll only for evening courses; day students can schedule some evening courses if it is more convenient. There is an orientation program for day and evening students, respectively, enrolled in each degree program.

II. Terminology

School of Continuing Education and Extension Services: a general way of indicating that a considerable range of activities will be found here that are found in other institutions by many other names. Continuing Education tends to mean non-credit courses, conferences, institutes, etc., especially for people who already have one or more college degrees, particularly professional ones.

III. Fees

There is no fee differential between day and evening credit courses. Students are charged a "flat" tuition rate because they schedule a "regular program."

IV. Faculty and Faculty Recruitment

It is against University rules for any member of any faculty to be used on an "overload" basis except in the School of Continuing Education and Extension Services or in Education Field Services or through a temporary ruling of the

New York University (cont.)

Chancellor. Faculty members are hired on recommendation
of the Dean to the Chancellor and the Board of Trustees.
Faculty meetings are held four times a year as established
by the Agenda Committee and additional faculty meetings are
sometimes called.

V. Scheduling

The Dean of the School of Continuing Education and
Extension Services is responsible for the schedule. The program administrator or department head turns in "room cards"
requesting space for his classes. After approval of the Curriculum Committee for any new courses or changes in fees,
etc., the recommendations are submitted to the Chancellor
and the Board of Trustees for formal approval. Most of the
classes are 2 hours (meeting once a week) or 4 hours (meeting twice a week). The few 3 hour classes are scheduled
once a week in the evening or twice a week in the daytime.
Research has been completed as follows: "A History of the
Division of General Education, New York University, 1934-
1959," Ed. D. Thesis submitted by Ann Freidus; "Patterns
of Educational Use of a Televised Public Affairs Program,
A Study of METROPOLIS: Creator or Destroyer," sponsored
by the University Council on Education for Public Responsibility. Study Director: Harry L. Miller; "New York University's Harlem Seminars," a narrative account of a Title I
(Higher Education Act of 1965) project under the direction of
Dr. Harry L. Miller; "Survey of University Adult Education
in the Metropolitan Area of New York," a study made possible by a grant from the Fund for the Advancement of Education, the Ford Foundation under the direction of Mrs. Caroline Ellwood; "An Evaluation of the MIND Adult Education
Center on West 114th Street in Harlem" an evaluation of a
novel attempt at prevocational basic education for residents
of 114th Street between 7th and 8th Avenues by MIND, Inc.,
a subsidiary of Corn Products Corporation. Evening classes
are better than day because they are taken by more interested students with a greater diversity of background. There
is no dean's list.

VI. General

The Division is experimenting with non-credit courses
for economically deprived students in off-campus locations.

There are many publications for faculty, both full and part-time, and also students. Approximately 50 special events will be open to faculty and students of our School, other schools of the University, and the general public. The Division is receiving adequate support in their undertakings. The Dean of the Division is responsible to the President and Chancellor of the University. There are about 200 special appearances on television and radio yearly as well as other instructional aids.

VII. Student Recruitment

There is an office concerned with publicity and information which is concerned with press releases, newspaper articles, radio and television appearances, etc. In addition to the general bulletin there are many brochures and fliers sent to students as well as industry and organizations. There is an Office of Special Services to Business and Industry.

*The Basic Core requirement for admission to special degree programs is high school graduation. Some adults are admitted on the basis of the adult admissions tests and others on SAT scores; in some cases they are admitted provisionally subject to the earning of an equivalency diploma within one calendar year.

* * *

Newark College of Engineering
Newark, New Jersey
Evening Sessions

Total enrollment 6, 465   Public Institution
Evening enrollment 3, 665   Semester System

I. Admission Policies

Deadline for application for admission for evening students is approximately one month prior to registration. Students may register without transcripts with a statement of good standing from the last college attended. A non-matriculated student is limited to one semester of work unless the credit is required at another school. Admission requirements for non-matriculating students is satisfactory completion of prerequisites; regular students must be high school graduates. Mail registration is used. Academic records of all evening students are reviewed by the Committee on Aca-

Newark College of Engineering (cont.)

demic Standing at the end of each spring semester. There is no special degree program for adults. Admission policies are set by the College's Executive Committee. Day and evening students may enroll in the same classes.

II.   Terminology

Title of Division: Evening Sessions, defined: Evening sessions (Undergraduate, Graduate, Division of Technology and Division of Continuing Engineering Studies) which covers the areas of responsibility for records, registration and schedules.

III.   Fees

Tuition is $14.00 per semester hour for irregular schedules and $12.00 for regular schedules. Refunds are made on a graduating percentage basis.

IV.   Faculty and Faculty Recruitment

Full-time regular faculty are encouraged to teach evening classes. Final authority to hire faculty lies with the Departments. Regular faculty meetings at the opening of the Fall Semester are held with the President; in addition, individual departments hold meetings as necessary through the year.

V.   Scheduling

The Director of the Evening Sessions is responsible for the evening class schedule. Three credit hour courses are one night a week in order to avoid "regular" students having a 5 evenings per week schedule. Part-time evening students are eligible for the Dean's List with 75% of a normal course load and a GPA of "3" or better out of "4" with no grade lower than "2."

VI.   General

The evening division is receiving adequate support. The Director of the Evening Sessions is responsible to the President.

162

VII. Student Recruitment

Newspaper advertisements for the Division of Technology are used. Posters for undergraduate and graduate sessions are used in appealing to industry; flyers for Continuing Engineering Studies are sent to Professional Societies.

* * *

Newark State College
Union, N. J.
Division of Field Services

| Total enrollment 3500 | Public Institution |
| Evening enrollment 6800 | Semester System |

I. Admission Policies

Deadlines for application for admission to evening classes: June 1 (fall), Nov. 1 (Spring), April 1 (Summer). A student may register for credit courses before transcripts are submitted. Non-matriculating or "special" students may take up to 16 sem. hrs. for credit before matriculating. There are no admission requirements for non-matriculating or "special" students. Regular students must be in the top 50% of their graduating class, must have a CEEB Verbal Score of 496 or above, and a 363 quantitative score. If a student selects to take the SCAT test, he must have a verbal score of 300 or above and a 290 quantitative score. Mail registration is available only to those students who are matriculated in degree programs. Retention policy--a 2. 0 average (C). Consideration is being given to offering a special degree program for adults. The college Admissions Committee formulates the admission policies for all students. Day students may enroll in the same class as evening students on a limited basis--it depends on space. Each student enrolling for evening classes is personally interviewed. The college has a 16 sem. hr. probationary program. These students are permitted to take a maximum of 16 sem. hrs. of prescribed liberal arts courses as a basis for reconsideration for admission.

II. Terminology

Title of Division: Division of Field Services. Defined: The major function of the division is to provide the best possible instruction and educational guidance for those

Newark State College (cont.)

who are to teach in New Jersey's schools. The division is
keenly aware of its responsibility for identifying and select-
ing students of high potential and seeks in every way possible
to attract to this institution persons of high professional
promise... Definition of Continuing Education: Continuing
Education in our view includes all programs--credit or non-
credit, which provide adults with the opportunity to continue
their educational objectives.

III. Fees

Day school students pay $350 tuition; evening students
pay $20 per credit undergraduate and $25 per credit graduate tuition. Refund policies; Withdrawal before semester
begins--100%; during first--third - 60%; between first and
third and first half - 30%; later - 0.

IV. Faculty and Faculty Recruitment

Approximately 66% of the faculty members teaching
evening classes are full-time. No full time faculty members
teach exclusively in the evening. The Director of the Division of Field Services is responsible for hiring full- and
part-time faculty members for evening classes in consultation with department chairmen. Faculty meetings for evening faculty are normally held once a semester, plus departmental meetings called by a departmental faculty member
who acts in a liaison capacity. The college does not ordinarily permit overloads for instructors, but frequent exceptions are made with the approval of the President.

V. Scheduling

The Director is responsible for the evening class
schedule. The schedule is based on previous enrollment
figures, classrooms available, number of sections required
and a cooperative effort between the evening staff and the
department chairmen. Most 3-hour classes are scheduled
one night per week with the exception of language and science
classes. Day and evening classes compare favorably in
quality. Part-time evening students are not eligible for the
Dean's List.

VI. General

The college offers credit and/or non-credit courses in off-campus locations for economically deprived populations. Students participate in discussions regarding the academic program through the Evening Division Honor Society and there is a "feedback" from the general student body. There could be more stress and financial support for the evening program, but the administration recognizes the need and importance of the adult education program. The Director is directly responsible to the President of the College.

VII. Student Recruitment

Newspaper stories and ads are used to publicize the adult education program, plus bulletins and flyers. No use is made of radio and television. Announcements are made to AAUW and to college clubs regarding special programs for adults.

* * *

University of North Carolina
Evening College
Chapel Hill, N. C.

Total enrollment 15, 500   Public Institution
Evening enrollment 650   Semester System

I. Admission Policies

The deadline for application for admission to evening classes coincides with the date for registration. Students may register for credit courses before transcripts are submitted, but all transcripts, confidential rating sheets, etc. must be in within three weeks. No work may be taken for credit as a "special" student. Regular students are admitted who score 800 or higher on the CEEB, and graduate in the 50th percentile or higher in their high school graduating class unless it has been over five years since they graduated from high school. Students are required to take placement tests in language, mathematics, etc. as part of the admissions process for placement and advisement. Regularly enrolled students whose programs have been approved by an advisor may register by mail. Retention policies: After 6 semester hours--1.00; after 12 semester hours--1.25; after 24 semester hours 1.50; after 36 semester hours--1.75; after 48 se-

165

mester hours--1. 90. A special degree program for adults is being considered for the near future. The Faculty Committee on Admissions formulates the admission policies for the evening students as well as for regular degree students. Evening College students may enroll in day classes with the approval of the Director of the Evening College and the Chairman of the Department. No Orientation Program is held for evening students.

II. Terminology

Title of Division: Evening College (a part of the College of Arts and Sciences administered by an official of the Extension Division). Defined: A general (two-year) program for adult students. Continuing Education defined: 1) as indicated above; 2) as synonymous with adult education, and 3) as adult education in one's professional or vocational field.

III. Fees

There is no fee differential between day and evening classes. Refund policy: "We charge one-tenth of the tuition for the course for each week attended; refund the remainder."

IV. Faculty and Faculty Recruitment

Approximately 5% of the evening faculty members are full-time. The Chancellor of the University has the final authority for hiring full and/or part-time faculty members for evening classes. No full-time faculty members teach exclusively in the evening. Faculty meetings are held for evening faculty once each semester. Regular faculty members may teach in the Evening College as part of their regular load, but not on an overload basis.

V. Scheduling

The Director of the Evening College has the responsibility for the evening class schedule, but as a matter of convenience, he "follows the regular University schedule." Staff members prepare the schedule for the Director's ap-

proval.   Three-hour classes are scheduled two nights a week
--with one or two exceptions.   Day and evening classes compare favorably in quality.   Part-time evening students are
not eligible for the Dean's List.

VI. General

Students participate in discussions regarding the academic program only on an informal basis.   The Evening College is receiving adequate stress and support from the administration.   The Director is responsible to the Dean of
Arts and Sciences and to the Director, Extension Division as
Associate Director of the Division.

VII.   Student Recruitment

The newspaper is used for promotion releases for
special programs.   Spot announcements are made on radio
and television regarding programs to be offered in the Evening College.   Brochures are prepared for distribution to industry and to various civic organizations and the Chamber
of Commerce.

*   *   *

Northeastern University
University College
Boston, Mass.

Total enrollment 35,000   Private Institution
Evening enrollment 12,500   Quarter System

I. Admission Policies

Deadline for application for admission to evening
classes: students must be enrolled before the second class
session.   A student may register for credit courses before
transcripts are submitted.   Unlimited hours may be taken as
a non-matriculating or "special" student.   Admission requirement for "special" students is high school graduation; for regular students--high school graduation plus maintenance of a
2.0 average.   Students may register by mail.   Currently,
all former students registered during the previous quarter
receive a packet of IBM forms and course information allowing them to register completely by mail.   Retention policies;
continual improvement in quality of program and faculty.
This institution has added 50 part-time academic counselors

167

to assist students in course selection and program planning. No ACT or CEEB scores are required for admission. Placement tests in English and Mathematics are given. The Academic Council (including the Dean of University College) formulates the admission policies for evening students. Day students may transfer evening credit with a grade of "C" or better. An Orientation Program is held for evening students during the first week of classes. All part-time students work toward a general Bachelor of Science degree.

II. Terminology

Title of Division: University College of Northeastern University. Defined: University College, so called because it draws upon the resources of the other colleges of the University, offers part-time programs in Liberal Arts, Business Administration, Law Enforcement and Security, and Health-Related Programs leading to the Associate in Science and Bachelor of Science degrees. Workshops and seminars are offered for degree credit.

III. Fees

There is a fee differential for students in the day and evening program. The reason is that part-time students are not eligible to participate in normal day social and academic activities. Tuition for any course is proportionally refundable until after the fifth session at which time the student is responsible for full course tuition.

IV. Faculty and Faculty Recruitment

There is no policy regarding the percentage of faculty for evening classes that must be full-time faculty members. At the present time, 20% of the liberal arts faculty is full-time; less than 1% of the faculty in business and management is full-time. The Dean of University College has the authority for hiring full and/or part-time faculty members for evening classes. Full-time faculty members are employed to teach exclusively in the evening. Faculty meetings for evening faculty are held in the early fall and late spring. The University College uses full-time faculty members on a limited basis and pays them for the overload.

V. Scheduling

The Dean of University College is responsible for the evening class schedule. Schedules are compiled by the program director in cooperation with the department consultant. As a result of University College's development in the past three years, the quality of evening classes is reaching a comparable level for both day and evening. Part-time evening students are not eligible for the Dean's List.

VI. General

Students participate very little in discussions regarding the academic program. The "Two Platoon System" is used for scheduling two courses per evening in the same classroom. More support could be given to the evening program including adequate stress and more financial support. The Dean of the University College is responsible directly to the Vice President and Dean of the Faculty.

VII. Student Recruitment

Extensive use is made of newspaper advertising. Approximately a million copies of a twelve-page Sunday Supplement is sent out just prior to fall registration. Spot announcements are made on the radio at registration time, and occasionally on television. Pamphlets and publications are prepared for business and industry.

* * *

Northern Illinois University
DeKalb, Ill.

Total enrollment 20, 719   Public Institution
Evening enrollment 3, 700   Semester System

I. Admission Policies

There is no deadline for applications for admission to evening classes except in Graduate School. Students may register for credit courses before transcripts are submitted. Non-matriculating or "special" students may take up to 12 sem. hrs. for credit before they are required to matriculate. High school graduation is required for admission as a "special" student. For regular students, they must be in the upper 50% of their graduating class. For Graduate School,

169

students must have earned a 2. 5 average for their last two
years as an undergraduate student. There is no mail registration. Scores on ACT or CEEB are not required for admission. The Admissions Committee formulates the admission policies for evening students. Day and evening students
may enroll in the same classes. No orientation program is
planned for evening students.

II. Terminology

Title of division: College of Continuing Education--
with Evening Division. Evening Division defined: A division
serving the part-time evening students on campus. Definition of Continuing Education: All types of formal and informal education taken after the completion of the uninterrupted
formal schooling.

III.   Fees

There is no fee differential between day and evening
classes. Students have 10 days to drop all courses with a
full refund.

IV.   Faculty and Faculty Recruitment

99% of the faculty teaching evening classes are full-
time, but no full-time faculty members teach exclusively in
the evening. The Department Heads and the Dean of the
College of Continuing Education have the responsibility for
hiring full and/or part-time faculty. No regular faculty
meetings are held for faculty teaching evening classes. Faculty members receive extra pay for an overload. They are
limited to the equivalent of one overload class per year.

V. Scheduling

The Dean of Continuing Education is responsible for
the evening class schedule. The departments initiate the
schedule of evening classes and the Dean approves. Most
3-hour classes are held one night per week with a few
classes meeting two nights per week. Evening classes are
equal or better in quality than day classes. Part-time eve-

ning students are not eligible for the Dean's List.

VI. General

Students do not participate in any discussions regarding the academic program. In general, the administration recognizes the need and importance of the evening program. The Dean of Continuing Education is responsible to the Provost.

VII. Student Recruitment

Newspaper ads and announcements are used for publicity, with announcements on radio and television. Special programs are planned for industry with publicity coverage.

* * *

Northern Virginia Community College
Bailey's Crossroads, Va.

Total enrollment 5, 188   Public Institution
Evening enrollment* 2017/1154   Quarter System
   *Includes day students taking
   one or more night courses

I. Admission Policies

There is no deadline for applications for admission to evening classes. Students may register for credit courses before transcripts are submitted. Non-matriculating or "special" students may take up to 45 quarter hours for credit before matriculating. Admission requirements for non-matriculating or "special" students: Applications for attendance, $5.00 application fee and registration for classes. Admission requirements for regular students: "Open-Door"--high school diploma or equivalency. No mail registration is used. Scores on ACT or CEEB are not required for admission. The Admissions Committee formulates the admission policies for all students. Day and evening students may enroll in the same class. No Orientation program is held for evening students.

II. Terminology

Title of Division: Continuing Adult Education and Community Services.

171

Northern Virginia Community College (cont.)

III. Fees

There is no fee differential between day and evening class enrollment. No refund is given after the first week of classes.

IV. Faculty and Faculty Recruitment

Approximately 20% of the faculty teaching evening classes is full-time. No full-time faculty members teach exclusively in the evening. Faculty meetings for evening faculty are held once quarterly. Full-time faculty members may teach an overload.

V. Scheduling

The Coordinator of Continuing Education and Community Services is responsible for scheduling evening classes in coordination with the Scheduling Committee and Department Coordinators. The schedule is submitted from Departments and Divisions, using "experience figures" from the previous quarter and adding additional courses. Three-hour classes are scheduled one night a week. Evening classes compare very favorably with day classes in quality with a "top-notch" part-time staff.

VI. General

More stress and financial support could be given to the evening program, but the administration recognizes the need and importance of the adult education program since the "objectives of the Community are clearly drawn to reflect emphasis on adult education." The Coordinator of Continuing Education and Community Services is responsible to the Dean of Instruction.

VII. Student Recruitment

All the media for publicity is used--newspaper stories and advertisements, radio and television announcements. Special motivational appeals are developed for business and

industry and for various civic organizations and the Chamber
of Commerce.

* * *

Northwestern University
Chicago, Illinois
Evening Divisions

Total enrollment 19,000 annually   Private Institution
Evening enrollment 8,000 annually   Semester System
4,300 current semester

I. Admission Policies

Deadline for application for admission is approximately two weeks before registration. Admission requirements
are high school graduation or 21 years of age and acceptable
other college transcripts. Students not interested in a degree may register for credit courses without transcripts and
may take a limited amount of credit work as non-matriculated students. Degree candidates must submit transcripts
if they have earned previous college credit. Mail registration is used for former students and is available to new students who have conferred with a counselor. Students with an
average below "C" are placed on probation and are excluded
if it is not maintained. Admission policies are set by the
Dean and his Advisory Council. Day and evening students
may enroll in the same classes. There is no orientation
program for evening students.

II. Terminology

Title of Division: Northwestern University Evening
Divisions, defined: The five day divisions are academically
responsible for their own evening programs, which are not
identical with day programs leading to degrees.

III. Fees

Evening students pay less than half the tuition day
students do; lab fees, etc., are exactly the same. Evening
students may use the full facilities of the university as day
students do.

Northwestern University (cont.)

IV. Faculty and Faculty Recruitment

25% teaching evening classes are full-time. Final authority to hire evening faculty lies with the Dean of the Evening Division. The Dean of the Evening Division can reject a faculty member assigned to teach evening classes and can engage an instructor without the consent of the department chairmen. Regular faculty meetings are not held. Faculty members may teach no more than one 4 credit hour course or two 2 credit hour courses on an overload basis during an academic year; this does not include non-credit courses.

V. Scheduling

The Dean of the Evening Divisions is responsible for the evening class schedule, and may revise it. The two-credit hour courses are scheduled each night of the week, Monday through Friday. Day and evening students are of similar quality; the best students, academically, are in the evening divisions as well as the worst. There is no Dean's List.

VI. General

Periodically the Dean meets with representative evening students to discuss the academic program. In general, the evening divisions are receiving adequate support. The Dean of the Evening Divisions is responsible to the Provost and Dean of Faculties. Audio-visual instructional aids are used in evening classes.

VII. Student Recruitment

Newspaper, radio and television publicity is used. Special motivational appeals have been developed for industry.

* * *

Ohio State University
Columbus, Ohio

Total enrollment 45,300   Public Institution
Evening enrollment 700   Quarter System

174

I. Admission Policies

Deadline dates for application for admission to evening classes: Aug. 1, November 15 and February 15. There is no separate evening college--only evening sections of regular classes. A student may register for credit courses before transcripts are submitted. Non-matriculating or "special" students may take an unlimited number of hours for credit. Admission requirements for non-matriculating or "special" students include high school graduation (no transcript required) and for regular students high school graduation with transcript. Scores for ACT or CEEB are not required for admission. Students may register by mail. Schedule cards may be mailed and returned by mail. If approved, fee cards are mailed and fees may be returned by mail. For retention, students must achieve basically a "C" average after 7 quarters of attendance. The Director of Admissions formulates the admission policies for evening students after consulting the division. No orientation program is held for evening students.

II. Terminology

Title of Division: Division of Continuing Education. Defined: In addition to special students who are formally enrolled, the division is involved in all non-credit courses offered throughout the university including Cooperative Extension, conferences, short courses, seminars, etc. Continuing Education defined: Any planned or organized learning process for the adult (excluding formal degree programs).

III. Fees

There is no fee differential between day and evening classes. Fees are based upon hours--1/2 fees for 6 hours or less; full fees for 7 hours or more. 50% refund up to 24 days into the quarter with maximum refund--90%.

IV. Faculty and Faculty Recruitment

There is no separate faculty for evening classes--with few exceptions, all faculty are full-time. Therefore, faculty members are hired by the respective day colleges within the university. No special faculty meetings are held for faculty members teaching in the evening. Overloads are permitted

Ohio State University (cont.)

for faculty. The amount is determined by the chairman of the particular department. There must be a formal supplemental appointment.

V. Scheduling

The Director of Continuing Education is not responsible for the evening class schedule. This is the responsibility of the Vice-President for Academic Affairs. Three-credit hour classes are scheduled one night per week. Day and evening classes are similar in quality. Part-time evening students are not eligible for the Dean's List.

VI. General

In general, the administration recognizes the need and the importance of the adult education program. The Director of Continuing Education is responsible to the Vice-President for Educational Services.

VII. Student Recruitment

Since there is no separate evening college, there is no special newspaper publicity for evening classes.

* * *

Old Dominion College*
Division of Continuing Education
Norfolk, Va.

Total enrollment 9, 300   Public Institution
Evening enrollment 3, 000   Semester System

I. Admission Policies

There is no deadline for application for admission. Students may register for credit courses without transcripts; however, official transcripts must be submitted within six weeks after start of classes. A non-matriculating student may take between 60 and 75 hours provided his transcripts are in order and he is in good standing. Admission requirements are graduation from high school or GED scores above

176

60 percentile in all areas. Students must maintain a "C"
average after completing 24 hours; suspension is for one full
academic year. There is no special degree program for
adults. Admission policies are set by the College Admissions Office in conjunction with the Division of Continuing
Education. Day students may enroll for as many evening
courses as they wish; evening and part-time students must
complete the major portion of their semester's work in the
evening hours. There is no orientation program for evening
students, however, the Division of Continuing Education publishes a Student Handbook and a bi-monthly, mimeographed
newspaper.

II. Terminology

Title of Division: Division of Continuing Education,
defined: Division in charge of resident, evening program,
extension program, public services and summer session.

III. Fees

Part-time undergraduate students pay $14 per credit
hour. Matriculated day students pay $200 per semester for
12-18 credits. Graduate fees are higher and include out-of-
state tuition fees. Evening students pay $14 per semester
hour. Refunds: withdrawal before beginning of classes--
full tuition minus a $5 registration fee; first week of classes
--2/3 refund; second week of classes--1/3 refund; after
second week--no refund, regardless of reason.

IV. Faculty and Faculty Recruitment

50% teaching evening classes are full-time faculty
members. Regular faculty generally teach only one course
at night and part-time instructors usually teach two courses
at night. Final authority to hire evening faculty lies with
Chairmen of Departments with approval of their academic
deans. Some full-time faculty members teach exclusively in
the evening. Teaching overloads for faculty are kept to an
absolute minimum.

V. Scheduling

The Dean of the Division of Continuing Education is
responsible for the evening class schedule. Evening classes

177

Old Dominion College* (cont.)

are listed in a special Evening College Brochure after being submitted to the Provost's Office. Part-time evening students are not listed on the Dean's List but the Evening College has an Honors Society. To qualify for the Honors Society, a student must have completed 18 credits or more at Old Dominion College with a quality point average of 3.5 or better (4 point system).

VI. General

Students participate in discussion regarding the academic program through the regularly scheduled meetings of the Honors Society. In addition, Evening College students have the opportunity to evaluate Evening College instruction through a specially prepared form, Students' Evaluation of Classroom Instruction.

*After Sept. 1, 1969 -- name will be changed to
Old Dominion University.

* * *

Orange County Community College
Middletown, N.Y.

Total enrollment 5,000   Public Institution
Evening enrollment 3,000   Semester System

I. Admission Policies

The deadline for application for admission to evening classes is the first week of classes. Students may register for credit courses before transcripts are submitted. Non-matriculating or "special" students may take an unlimited number of courses, provided they maintain acceptable grades. The admission requirement for non-matriculating students is high school diploma or equivalency. For regular students, the SUNY Admissions Examination is required plus a high school diploma and the guidance counselor's recommendation. Students may register by mail from the fifth week preceding the beginning date of classes up to the second week. Retention policies: Varies dependent on grade point after 12 credit hours; dismissal or suspension if less than 1.75 after two semesters. The ACT or CEEB is not required. A special degree program for adults is being considered. The admissions requirements are formulated by the registrar's office and admissions office jointly for evening students. Day and evening students may enroll in the same class. Evening students may attend the orientation program for full-time students held during the day.

II. Terminology

Title of Division: Division of Continuing Education, defined: Credit and non-credit courses offered after 4:30 p. m. (on and off-campus) and special interest courses.

III. Fees

There is a fee differential between full-time and part-time students. Full-time students (in-state) pay $200 and a $20 activity fee; part-time students (in-state) pay $13 per credit hour. Refund policies: less than two weeks after the semester begins--75%; 2-4 weeks--50%; after 4 weeks--no refunds.

IV. Faculty and Faculty Recruitment

Approximately 50% of the faculty for evening classes are full-time faculty members. The Director of Continuing Education has the final authority for hiring full and/or part-time faculty members for evening classes. No full-time faculty members teach exclusively in the evening. Faculty meetings are held once a year. Faculty members receive a separate salary for overloads dependent on rank; they are responsible to the Division Chairmen and the Director of Continuing Education.

V. Scheduling

The Director of Continuing Education is responsible for the evening class schedule together with the recommendations of the various divisions and areas of interest. Each division recommends credit and non-credit courses; the Assistant Director of Continuing Education recommends off-campus and non-credit courses. Most 3 hour classes are scheduled one night a week. A research project has been completed on a "Five-Year Prediction of Continuing Education Programs

Orange County Community College (cont.)

at Orange County Community College" by Howard C. Smith, Jr. Day and evening classes are equal in terms of quality. Parttime evening students are not eligible for the Dean's List.

VI. General

Credit and non-credit courses at off-campus locations are offered for economically deprived populations in four major locations and on a collegiate bus. Students are appointed to all committees, including the academic policy committee. The Division of Continuing Education is receiving adequate stress and financial support from the administration. The Director of Continuing Education is responsible to the Academic Dean and the President.

VII. Student Recruitment

The college uses full-page ads listing courses every semester in the local newspaper. Scheduled paid announcements are heard on radio and also on CATV. The college sponsors in-plant training programs for industry and representatives of the college serve on advisory committees for various civic organizations and the Chamber of Commerce. Guest speakers are available for civic clubs.

* * *

Pace College
New York, N.Y.

Total enrollment 9,200   Private Institution
Evening enrollment 4,900   Semester System

I. Admission Policies

There is no deadline for application for admission to evening classes. Students may register for credit courses before transcripts are submitted. "Special" students may take as many as 30 sem. hrs. before matriculating. Admission requirements for "special" students include high school graduation and a minimum high school average of 70. Admission requirements for regular students include high school graduation with 11 academic units and a minimum of 78 high school average. Students must make a minimum score of 850 on the SAT. No mail registration is used. No special degree program for adults is now being offered. The administrative committee formulates the admission policies for all students. Day and evening students may enroll in the same class subject to space limitations. An Orientation Program is scheduled two weeks after the start of the semester.

II. Terminology

Title of Division: No special designation. Each school offers day and evening programs. The School of Continuing Education is intended for non-matriculation and special students. Definition of Continuing Education: Course work to qualify for matriculation and courses for those desiring to fulfill only limited educational objectives, e. g. just courses in art or in accounting.

III. Fees

1/3 of the faculty teaching evening classes are full-time faculty members. Some full-time faculty members teach exclusively in the evening. The Dean has the final authority for hiring full and part-time faculty members with the concurrence of the Academic Vice President. Faculty meetings are held for evening faculty members at the start of the academic year. Faculty members are permitted to carry an overload.

V. Scheduling

The Institutional Research Office is responsible for the evening class schedule. The evening class schedule is compiled after the preliminary registration and with consultation with the registrar, and Departmental Chairmen. 3-hour classes are scheduled to meet two nights per week. Day and evening classes compare favorably in quality. Part-time evening students are eligible for the Dean's List by attaining an average of 24/3 on 12 hrs.

VI. General

Credit and non-credit courses are offered in off-campus locations for economically deprived populations. Three student members are included on the Curriculum Planning Committee. Adequate stress and financial support is

Pace College (cont.)

given to the evening program.

VII. Student Recruitment

Announcements and news stories appear in the newspapers, and spot announcements are prepared for radio and television. Business and industry are informed about the academic program and special course offerings. Contact is made with various civic organizations concerning the evening program.

* * *

Peirce Junior College
Philadelphia, Pa.

Total enrollment 1, 200   Private Institution
Evening enrollment 800   Semester System

I. Admission Policies

Deadlines for application for admission to evening classes; September 19 (fall); February 13 (spring). Students may register for credit courses before transcripts are submitted. "Special" students may take a maximum of 12 hours for credit before matriculation. Admission requirements for non-matriculating or "special" students--high school graduation. Admission requirements for regular students--high school graduation. Mail registration is not used. ACT or CEEB scores are not required for admission. The Associate in Arts Degree is offered for adults with 500 students enrolled in the degree program. The Admissions Committee formulates the admission policies for evening students. Evening Division Classes are also offered in the day college. No Orientation program is held for evening students.

II. Terminology

Title of Division: Evening Division. Continuing Education includes both continuing programs for adults and degree programs.

III. Fees

There is a fee differential for day and evening stu-

182

dents. Refund policy: Minimum tuition retained, first or
second week--20%; third week--30%; fourth week--40%; fifth
week--60%; sixth week--80%; seventh and thereafter--none.

IV. Faculty and Faculty Recruitment

50% of the faculty teaching evening classes are full-
time. Some full-time faculty members teach exclusively in
the evening. The Director of the Evening Division (who is
also Dean of Instruction) has the final authority for hiring
full- and part-time faculty members for evening classes.
No regular faculty meetings are held for evening faculty.
Day faculty members are permitted to teach six hours in the
evening as an overload.

V. Scheduling

The Director of the Evening Division is responsible
for the evening class schedule. Classes are scheduled one
night a week. Part-time evening students are eligible for
the Dean's List by taking 12 hours with a 3.5 grade point
average (no grades lower than "C"). In general, adequate
stress and financial support is given to the evening program.
The Director of the Evening Division is responsible to the
Vice-President of Academic Affairs.

VII. Student Recruitment

Newspaper ads and special announcements are used
for publicity purposes. Special programs are offered for
business and industry and publicity material is sent to civic
organizations and the Chamber of Commerce.

* * *

Philadelphia College of Textiles and Science
Evening College
Philadelphia, Pa.

Total enrollment 1081   Private Institution
Evening enrollment 818   Semester System

I. Admission Policies

Deadline dates for applications for admission: September 16 and January 17. A student may not register for

Philadelphia Coll. of Textiles & Science (cont.)

credit courses before transcripts are submitted. "Special" students may take as many as 60 sem. hrs. for credit before matriculating. Admission for "special" students includes having the pre-requisites for the course. Admission requirements for regular students includes high school graduation with the required subjects, entrance examinations or an official transcript from the college previously attended. No mail registration is used. A "C" average is required for retention. No ACT or CEEB scores are required for admission. No special degree program for adults is available. The Dean of the Evening College formulates the admission policies for evening students. Day and evening students may enroll in the same classes. An orientation program is held at the beginning of each semester. The college has been enrolling more transfer students than "new" students the past two or three years.

II. Terminology

Title of Division: Evening College. Defined: A college with a separate faculty and student body which schedules classes from 7:00 p. m. - 9:45 p. m.

III. Fees

A smaller fee is charged evening students to meet competition from other institutions. Refund policies: 70%-- 1st week; 50% second week; 0 after the second week.

IV. Faculty and Faculty Recruitment

40% of the faculty of 81 members are full-time. No full-time faculty member teaches exclusively in the evening. The Dean of the Evening College has the final authority for hiring full- and part-time faculty. Faculty meetings for evening faculty are held once a year. Overloads are limited to one three-hour course or the equivalent.

V. Scheduling

The Dean of the Evening College is responsible for the evening class schedule. Classes are scheduled to meet the need of students. The quality of evening classes compared to day classes varies--some are very good and others somewhat inferior. Part-time students are eligible for the Dean's List by taking 9 hours with a 3. 33 average based on 4. 00.

VI. General

Students are included on the Curriculum and Student Affairs Committees, and students have an opportunity to discuss matters relating to the academic program. Adequate stress and financial support is given to the evening program. The Dean is responsible to the President of the College.

VII. Student Recruitment

Special newspaper ads are prepared three times per year as well as spot announcements on the radio. Brochures are sent to business and industrial concerns on special courses offered for business and industry.

* * *

Polytechnic Institute of Brooklyn
Brooklyn, N. Y.
Evening Session

Total enrollment 2392 (Undergr.)   Private Institution
2700 (Grad.)   Semester System
Evening enrollment 634 (Undergr.)
2200 (Graduate)

I. Admission Policies

The published deadline for application for admission to evening classes: August 1 and January 1, but the deadlines are not rigidly followed. Students may not register for credit courses without a transcript. "Special" students may take unlimited courses for credit. Admission requirements for all students includes 18 high school units including English 4/ Mathematics 3-1/2/ Chemistry 1/ Physics 1. All students must be high school graduates. Mail registration is used. Continuing students may request registration by mail by filing an advance approval listing courses desired. Evening students must maintain a 2. 00 ("C") average. ACT or CEEB scores are not required for admission. The Director of Admissions formulates the admission policies for evening students. Day and evening students may enroll in

185

the same classes. No Orientation Program is planned for evening students.

II. Terminology

Title of Division: Evening Session. Definition: Classes scheduled from 6:00-10:00 p. m. Definition of Continuing Education: That work which is taken beyond the baccalaureate level regardless of credit status.

III. Fees

There is a fee differential for day and evening classes. Day session--$65/credit; evening session--$55/credit.

IV. Faculty and Faculty Recruitment

65% of the faculty teaching evening classes are fulltime. The Department Heads have the authority for hiring full- or part-time faculty members. No full-time faculty members teach exclusively in the evening. No regular faculty meetings are held for evening faculty. Full-time faculty members are required to teach in the Evening Session as part of their normal load. No overload status is available.

V. Scheduling

The department heads and registrar are responsible for the evening class schedule. Student requests are considered in determining the evening schedule. Three-hour classes are scheduled two nights per week. Day and evening classes are considered equal in quality. Part-time evening students are eligible for a separate Dean's List for evening students by taking at least 12 credits per year with a 3.00 average.

VI. General

Students participate in discussions regarding the academic program through the Student-Faculty Alumni Committee. Adequate stress and financial support is given to the evening program. The Dean of Students is directly responsible to the President.

VII. Student Recruitment

Newspaper ads and special announcements are used for publicity purposes. Special programs are offered for business and industry.

* * *

Pratt Institute
Brooklyn, N. Y.
School of Continuing Professional Studies

Total enrollment 4, 500   Private Institution
Evening enrollment: Semester System
   350 in Building Science
   250 in Non-credit Programs

I. Admission Policies

Deadline for application for admission to evening classes coincides with the registration date. Students may register for credit courses before transcripts are submitted because all students are non-matriculated until 18 semester hours of work are completed at Pratt. "Special" students may take a maximum of 18 semester hours for credit before matriculation. Admission requirements for "special" students includes the ability to meet standards of the particular course. Regular students must have a high school diploma or its equivalent. No ACT or CEEB scores are required for admission. Mail registration is used for upper class or returning students only. Retention policy: Maintenance of satisfactory academic point average. Department evening tests are given in some areas. The overall Institute policy for admission is determined by the Academic Council. Day and evening students do not normally enroll in the same classes. An Orientation program for evening students is planned. The Institute strongly believes in a procedure of using a validation process requiring stated number of hours to be completed meeting a stated standard before degree candidacy is established.

II. Terminology

Title of Division: Division of Building Science and

187

Pratt Institute (cont.)

Division of Continuing Education--both Divisions within The
School of Continuing Professional Studies. Defined: Applies
to formal credit programs for adults (students working at
full-time day position) and non-credit professional programs
unrestricted as to age or background. Continuing Education
defined: Basically programs either credit or non-credit
which seek to provide additional education to meet existing
need of the individual being served and at no specified age
level.

III. Fees

There is no fee differential between day and evening
classes. Refund policy: Standard practice based on percentage refund up through 5th week of classes.

IV. Faculty and Faculty Recruitment

No more than 10% of the faculty teaching evening
classes are full-time. No full-time faculty members teach
exclusively in the evening. The Dean of the School has the
final authority for hiring full- and part-time faculty members. Faculty meetings are held for evening faculty members in the fall and the spring. Faculty members may carry
an overload if desired.

V. Scheduling

The Divisional Director is responsible for the evening
class schedule subject to the approval of the Dean of the
School. Three-hour classes are held once a week. Day and
evening classes are comparable "to the extent that factors of
age and experience are weighted into the analysis." Part-
time evening students are eligible for the Dean's List by taking 8 hours with a GPA of 3.0.

VI. General

Students have an opportunity to participate in discussions regarding the academic program through elected student representatives who serve on the Curriculum Committee for the Division and also on the Planning Committee.

The evening program is receiving adequate stress and financial support by the administration. The Divisional Directors (Building Science and Continuing Education) report to the Dean of the School of Continuing Professional Studies, and the Dean reports directly to the Vice-President for Academic Affairs.

VII. Student Recruitment

The School uses the newspaper for publicity purposes, but not the radio or television. Special contact is made with business and industry concerning programs of interest to their personnel.

* * *

Purdue University
Calumet Campus
Hammond, Ind.

Total enrollment 3, 997   Public Institution
Evening enrollment 2, 260   Semester System

I. Admission Policies

Students may apply for admission through the late registration period. Students may register for credit courses before transcripts are submitted. Non-matriculating or "special" students may take up to 11 hours for credit before matriculating. Admission requirements for "special" students: Ability to handle the course work. Regular students must have graduated in the upper 1/2 of their class or should be in the upper 1/2 of the national average of the SAT. No mail registration is used. The CEEB is required for regular students and CEEB Achievement tests are used for placement purposes. The University Board of Trustees formulates the admission policies for all students. Day and Evening students may enroll in the same classes. There is no Orientation for evening students, but they may attend day Orientation. The evening program is a continuation and extension of the regular collegiate activity at the campus.

II. Terminology

Title of Division: No distinct and separate division for the evening college. Definition of Continuing Education: Continuing Education may be formal or informal. It may in-

189

Purdue University (cont.)

volve credit or non-credit, but in any event it serves the student by providing him with information, knowledge, or cultural values which enhance his ability to earn a living, his zeal for living, or his role as a member of society.

III. Fees

All fees are charged on a per credit hour basis. Refund policies: 1st week of classes--100% refund, 2nd week of classes--60% refund, 3rd week of classes--40% refund, 4th week of classes--20%, thereafter--0.

IV. Faculty and Faculty Recruitment

Budgetarily 25% of the evening classes are covered as a part of the regular teaching load of full time faculty. Usually somewhat more are included in the teaching faculty for evening classes. The Dean and Director of the Calumet Campus of the University have the final authority for hiring full- and part-time faculty members. Recruitment of part-time faculty is delegated to the Chairmen of the various departments. Regular faculty members do not now receive overload payments for participating in non-credit Continuing Education activities. This policy is presently up for review.

V. Scheduling

The Dean and Director of the Calumet Campus of the University has the final responsibility for all class schedules. Information is compiled from the various departments for all parts of the schedule both day and evening. This information is assembled and much of the requirements for the schedule are put together by the Assistant Dean for Academic Affairs in cooperation with the Assistant Director for Administration who is in charge of space use. Day and evening classes are judged on the same standard and taught according to the same standards. Part-time students are highly motivated. Part-time evening students are eligible for the Dean's List by accumulating 12 hours with grades of "B" or above.

VI. General

Students participate in discussions regarding the academic program by means of offering suggestions to the faculty and the administration. The administration recognizes the importance of adult education and gives adequate stress and support to the program. The Dean and Director of the Calumet Campus is responsible to a Vice-President for Regional Campus Administration.

VII. Student Recruitment

The newspaper is used for periodic advertising and news releases. New releases are given to radio and television. A number of specific bulletins are published by the University putting particular stress on technical programs and special cultural events which are distributed as seen fit to industry, to libraries, to school systems, through chambers of commerce, and to local organizations.

* * *

Queensborough Community College
Evening and General Studies Division
Bayside, N. Y.

Total enrollment 8, 700   Public Institution
Evening enrollment 5, 200   Semester System

I. Admission Policies

Deadline for application for matriculation for degree students is same as for day students. Non-matriculated students have no deadline and may register for credit courses without transcripts. Mail registration is used only for non-credit courses and off-campus courses. Matriculated degree students must maintain 1. 3 after 6-11-1/2 credits; 1. 5 with 12-27 credits; 1. 7 with 28-44 credits; 1. 9 with 45-63 credits; 2. 0 with 64+ credits. Placement tests are given to adults in the evening division and results are used for advising. A special degree for adults is being considered. Admission policies for matriculated evening students are set by the faculty committees, for non-degree students by the Dean of the Evening and General Studies Division. Day and evening students may enroll in the same classes with permission. There is no orientation for evening students.

Queensborough Community College (cont.)

II. Terminology

Title of Division: Evening and General Studies Division, defined: A division of the College with the following areas of responsibility: Evening session, Adult-Continuing Education Program, Community Service Program, Basic Educational Skills Training Program and an Urban Center (when developed).

III. Fees

Matriculated students do not pay tuition, non-matriculated students pay $15 per semester hour. Refunds are made to students on the following basis: before first class-- 100%; first week--75%; second week--50%; third week--25%; after third week--none.

IV. Faculty and Faculty Recruitment

Approximately 5% teaching evening classes are full-time. Final authority to hire evening faculty lies with the president of the college. Some full-time faculty members teach exclusively in the evening. Regular faculty meetings are held in the fall. If and when it is necessary for a faculty member to teach on an overload basis, he receives extra compensation.

V. Scheduling

The Dean of the Evening Division is responsible for the evening class schedule. The Dean has the authority to revise or change the evening schedule. Three credit hour classes are held two nights a week. Part-time evening students are eligible for the Dean's List with a 3.0 after completing 15 credits.

VI. General

Students are on most committees and participate in discussion regarding the academic program. In general, all evening divisions are not receiving adequate support. The Dean of the Evening and General Studies Division is responsible to the President of the College. All audio-visual instructional aids are available for evening classes.

VII. Student Recruitment

Newspaper advertisements in all New York papers are used. Special motivational appeals have been developed for industry and civic organizations.

* * *

The University of Richmond
Richmond, Virginia
University College
Total enrollment 6, 000+   Private, Church-related
Evening enrollment 1, 623   Institution
                                            Semester System

I. Admission Policies

There is no deadline for application for admission to evening classes; only registration deadlines. With the Dean's permission, some students may register for credit courses without transcripts. Admission requirements are high school graduation or in good standing at last college attended. Mail registration is used. If a student receives five failing grades, he is dropped from "credit" work. Special degrees for adults: Bachelor of Arts, Bachelor of Commerce, Master of Commerce, Master of Humanities. Admission requirements for the special degrees are successful completion of 45 hours. Admission policies are set by the full-time evening faculty and the Dean. Day students may register for evening classes with special permission. There is no orientation for evening students.

II. Terminology

Title of Division: University College, defined: A University within a University (not a college) and oriented toward the community.

III. Fees

Day students pay $140 per three hour undergraduate course; evening students pay $54 per three hour undergraduate course. Refunds are made to students only for reason of draft or sickness.

The University of Richmond (cont.)

IV. Faculty and Faculty Recruitment

25% teaching evening classes are full-time. Final authority to hire full-time faculty members lies with the President, part-time members with the Dean. The Dean of University College can reject a faculty member assigned to teach evening classes. The full-time evening faculty members who teach exclusively in the evening are responsible to the Dean of University College. Regular faculty meetings are held with evening faculty twice a month. Faculty members may teach one (3 credit hour) course on an overload basis, with permission.

V. Scheduling

The Dean of University College is responsible for the evening class schedule, and has the authority to revise and make additions to it. Three credit hour courses are scheduled one night a week. Day and evening classes are equal in terms of quality. Part-time evening students are not eligible for the Dean's List.

VI. General

The evening division is receiving adequate support. The Dean of University College is responsible to the President. Complete audio-visual instructional aids are available for evening classes.

VII. Student Recruitment

Newspaper publicity is used.

* * *

Roanoke College
Salem, Va.

Total enrollment 1,096   Private Church-related
   (195 in special courses)   Institution
Evening enrollment 478   Semester System
   (plus 195)

194

I. Admission Policies

Deadline for application for admission to evening classes is prior to the second week of classes. Deadline dates: September 18, (Fall) and February 5 (Spring). Students may register in credit courses for non-credit without transcripts. "Special" students may take a maximum of 21 hours before matriculating as degree students. Admission requirements for "special" students include a high school or college transcript or "Certificate." Regular students are required to submit a $15 application fee, picture, and transcripts. CEEB scores are required for day students, with a score of 500 on the verbal and mathematics test. Mail registration is used for returning students. Retention policies: C- --one year; C av. --second year; C+ average-- third and fourth year. Placement tests in mathematics and English are required. The Dean, Director of Admissions and the Director of Continuing Education formulate the admission policies for the evening students. Day and evening students may enroll in the same classes. No orientation program is offered for evening students.

II. Terminology

Title of Division: Evening Program and Continuing Education. Defined: This office takes care of evening classes. The Continuing Education was added to take care of non-credit educational activities--seminars, conferences, institutes, business and industrial education. Continuing Education defined: Credit and non-credit work offered by business and industry, high schools, colleges, correspondence education which is beyond a normal educational program according to age.

III. Fees

There is a fee differential for day and evening students--$132.50 for day students; $66 for evening students for three credits per semester. Refund policy: 80% refund during the first week of classes; no refund after that time.

IV. Faculty and Faculty Recruitment

40% of the faculty teaching evening classes is full-time. No full-time faculty members teach exclusively in the

Roanoke College (cont.)

evening. The Dean of the College has the final authority for hiring full- and part-time faculty. Faculty meetings are held for evening faculty on the first night of class each evening during the first week. Faculty members are paid extra for teaching an overload, but they cannot go beyond 15 total hours. The regular teaching load is 12 hours.

V. Scheduling

The Director of the Evening Program and Continuing Education is responsible for the evening class schedule. The evening class schedule attempts to meet the needs of students earning the degree and also to meet the special needs of the community. 95% of the evening classes meet one night a week. Classes in languages, sciences, freshmen English and mathematics meet two nights a week. Evening classes are considered superior to day classes. Part-time evening students are not eligible for the Dean's List.

VI. General

The college offers credit and non-credit courses in off-campus locations for economically deprived populations including Headstart and Upward Bound students. Students have the opportunity to participate in discussions regarding the academic program with non-voting membership on faculty committees. More stress and support could be given to the evening program. The Director of the Evening Program is responsible to the Dean and the President.

VII. Student Recruitment

Newspaper stories and announcements are used for publicity purposes as well as radio and television in public service programs. Business and industry are contacted directly and special brochures are sent to various companies concerning special courses and programs relating to business and industry. The staff is available to speak to civic clubs and various other organizations regarding special programs and courses.

* * *

Rochester Institute of Technology
College of Continuing Education
Rochester, N. Y.

Total enrollment 15,000   Private Institution
Evening enrollment 10,500   Semester System

I. Admission Policies

The deadline for application for admission to evening
classes is one week after the beginning of classes. Students
may register for credit courses before transcripts are submitted. "Special" students may take 12 hours before matriculation is permitted. Admission requirements for "special"
students include interest in the course and possession of prerequisites stated in the catalog. Regular students are required to have a high school diploma (except for non-degree
credit). Mail registration is used--Rochester Institute of
Technology was one of the first institutions to use mail registration. Retention policies: first four semesters in any
degree program--1.8 out of 4.0. Fifth semester and to completion, 2.0. Non-degree or "special" students must maintain a "D" grade in diploma level courses. In degree classes,
they must meet standards as indicated above. ACT or CEEB
scores are not required for admission--do not believe scores
are valid. Students do take a mathematics placement test
where appropriate. The Associate in Arts degree is offered
for adults with an enrollment of 150 students, about 60 working towards the degree. Admission requirement for this degree is 25 years or older. The program will be enlarged
to include a broad emphasis on Fine Arts as well as General Education. The Directors Committee formulates the admission policies for the evening students with the approval
by the Central Committee of the College of Continuing Education. Day students may enroll in evening classes for
make-up, to avoid schedule conflicts and for enrichment.
Evening students, transferred to night work, may enroll in
day classes for not more than two years. No Orientation
program is offered for evening students. Additional comments: We have what is known as an open admissions policy
which results in an attrition no greater than the restrictive
admissions of the day programs. However, many students
at night take several courses before they decide on matriculation which would invalidate this claim.

II. Terminology

Title of Division: College of Continuing Education.

197

Rochester Institute of Technology (cont.)

Defined: Any program not part of the day program except where NSF grant is involved. Also includes day programs in the Summer Session. Continuing Education in general includes any educational activity which follows the point at which the individual had considered his education terminal and which he pursues when an adult. An adult may be defined as anyone over 16 or who has completed high school.

III. Fees

There is no fee differential for students enrolled in day or in evening classes. Refund policy is on a graduated basis.

IV. Faculty and Faculty Recruitment

About 12% of the faculty teaching evening classes are full-time. Some full-time faculty members teach exclusively in the evening. The Dean delegates authority for hiring full- and part-time faculty to the Assistant Dean. Faculty meetings for the evening faculty are held in the fall and spring. Full-time faculty members receive extra compensation for teaching evening classes as an overload.

V. Scheduling

The Dean has the responsibility for the evening class schedule, but most of the work is done by the Assistant Dean and the Registrar. The class schedule has evolved over many years and is revised only insofar as necessary to make it possible for degree or diploma students to schedule their classes on the most convenient nights. Most three-hour classes are scheduled two evenings per week. In comparing day and evening classes, the following remarks were made by the Dean of the College of Continuing Education: "The graduate record examination is administered to all graduates in Mechanical and Electrical Engineering. While there has been no significant difference, evening student grades have been higher although the range is greater. In accounting we participate in the national accounting tests and equal, or better, the day student scores." Part-time evening students are eligible for the Dean's List by accumulating 12 hours per year with a 3.2 average."

VI. General

The Student President (Day) sits on the Policy Committee and the Student President (Evening) sits on the Central Committee to voice student opinion on the academic program. Rochester Institute of Technology is just beginning to
use closed circuit TV both day and evening. "We have an
IBM 1500 computer available to all, but specifically for students of the National Technical Institute for the Deaf. The
evening program generally receives adequate stress and financial support. The Dean of the College of Continuing Education is responsible to the Vice President for Academic
Administration.

VII. Student Recruitment

Newspaper ads and special announcements are used
for publicity purposes, but radio and television are not used.
Special announcements are made to business and industry,
and to like organizations, concerning programs of interest to
industry and special groups.

* * *

Rockford Evening College
Rockford, Ill.

Total enrollment 1, 498   Private Institution
Evening enrollment 879   Semester System

I. Admission Policies

The deadline for application for admission to evening
classes is the opening of the semester. Students may register for credit courses before transcripts are submitted.
"Special" students may take up to 60 semester hours for credit before matriculation. Admission requirements for "special"
students include Certification of high school graduation (special form). Regular students must submit a high school
transcript. No ACT or CEEB scores are required for admission. Students must maintain a "C" average. The Admissions Committee of the Day College formulates the admission policies for evening students upon recommendation of
the evening staff. Day students may enroll for one evening
class with no restrictions on how many day students are in
each class. No Orientation program is held for evening students.

Rockford Evening College (cont.)

II. Terminology

Title of Division: Evening College. Defined: Adult program for part-time students. Definition of Continuing Education: Any formal education taken by persons over 21-- seminars, short courses, regular courses for credit or non-credit.

III. Fees

There is a fee differential for day and evening students; Day--$40 per credit hour; Evening--$25 per credit hour. No special services are provided for evening students who come to the campus for one evening class a week. Refund policy: A graduated percentage during the first three weeks of a semester.

IV. Faculty and Faculty Recruitment

Approximately 30% of the faculty teaching evening classes are full-time. The departmental chairmen have the final authority for hiring full- and part-time members. Some full-time faculty members teach exclusively in the evening. Faculty meetings are held for evening faculty at the beginning of each semester. Overloads are permissible for faculty members with permission given by the chairman of the department. Extra remuneration is given for overloads.

V. Scheduling

The Dean of the Evening College is responsible for the evening class schedule. The Dean confers with the departmental chairmen in compiling the evening schedule of classes. Three-hour classes are scheduled on one night per week. According to the Dean, the evening classes are excellent-- they are sometimes superior to day classes. No Dean's List is used at the college.

VI. General

Once a year, 40 students are selected at random from those anticipating graduation in the next 12-18 months to discuss the academic program at the college. More adequate stress and financial support could be given to the Evening College, although the administration recognizes the need and the importance of the adult education program. The Dean of the Evening College is responsible to the President.

VII. Student Recruitment

The college places special advertisements and announcements in the newspaper for publicity purposes, and spot announcements are prepared for radio. Very little use is made of television for publicity. Special posters are distributed to business and industry.

* * *

Roosevelt University
Chicago, Ill.
Division of Continuing Education

Total enrollment 7, 000   Private Institution
Evening enrollment 3, 000   Semester System

I. Admission Policies

Deadlines for application for admission to evening classes: October 1 (Fall); February 10 (Spring) and June 23 (Summer). A student may register for credit courses before transcripts are submitted on a tentative basis. "Special" students may take a maximum of 30 semester hours for credit. Admission requirements for "special" students include a 2.0 average for transfer students--upper half of class; ACT, SAT or entrance examination and high school diploma. Regular students must have a high school diploma and ACT, SAT or Roosevelt University Entrance Examinations. Evening students are not required to take the ACT or CEEB, but do take the Roosevelt University Entrance Examinations. No mail registration is used. A special degree program for adults is available--a Bachelor of General Studies with an enrollment of 550 students. The same admission requirements apply as those for regular students. The Director of Admissions and Administrative Council formulate the admission policies for evening students. Day and evening students may enroll in the same classes. No Orientation program is held for evening students.

Roosevelt University (cont.)

II. Terminology

Title of Division: Division of Continuing Education.
Definition: The division has charge of extension programs
and the adult degree program together with non-credit vocational programs in the evening.

III. Fees

There is no fee differential for day and evening students. Refund policies: 80%--1st week; 60%--second week;
40%--3rd week; 20%--4th week. Beyond the 4th week--no
refund.

IV. Faculty and Faculty Recruitment

The Dean of Arts and Sciences has the final authority
for hiring full- and part-time faculty. No full-time faculty
teach evening classes exclusively. Faculty meetings are held
for evening faculty membes periodically. No overloads are
permitted for faculty.

V. Scheduling

The Dean of Arts and Sciences and department heads
are responsible for the evening class schedule. Three-hour
classes are scheduled either one or two nights per week depending on the subject. Part-time evening students are eligible for the Dean's List after completing fifteen hours.

VI. General

Students have little opportunity to participate in discussions regarding the academic program. The Director of
the Division of Continuing Education is responsible to the
Dean of Faculties.

VII. Student Recruitment

Newspaper articles and advertisements are used for
publicity purposes. Contacts are made with business and
industry and with civic organizations.

202

Rutgers University
University College

Total enrollment 26,234   Public Institution
Evening enrollment 7,812   Semester System

I. Admission Policies

Deadline for application for admission to evening
classes is about a month before registration: students may
not register for credit courses without transcripts.   A student may take a maximum of 30 hours as a non-matriculating student.   Admission requirements: upper 3/4 of high
school class or GED; good standing from another college.
Mail registration is used.   All students receive registration
material by mail; return is approximately 60%.   Students
must maintain averages as specified by the faculty committee on scholastic standing.   No special degree program for
adults offered and not considered.   Admission policies are
set by a faculty committee on admissions.   Day and evening
students may register in the same classes.   There is an
orientation program for evening students during the fall and
spring terms.

II. Terminology

Title of Division: University College, defined: A
college within the framework of the University.   Continuing
Education, defined: a sequential educational program designed to assist mature students in their ability to communi-
cate, to discharge responsibility to self and society, to use
the processes of thinking, appreciation and to develop the
habit of self-education for continued self improvement.

III. Fees

Day students are charged on a term basis; evening
students on a credit hour basis.   Refunds are made partially
in diminishing percentages up to eight weeks after the term
begins.

IV. Faculty and Faculty Recruitment

30% of the faculty teaching evening classes are full-
time.   The final authority for hiring faculty lies with the department chairmen with certification by the dean; faculty members
are responsible to the dean.   Faculty meetings are held in the

Rutgers University (cont.)

spring and fall and on demand of the faculty or dean. Faculty are limited to the equivalent of four semester hours per term as an overload.

V. Scheduling

The Dean of University College is responsible for the schedule. Three credit hour classes are scheduled only two nights per week. Part-time students are eligible for the Dean's List after completing 12 hours with a 1.90 or better.

VI. General

The University College offers tutorial and remedial programs on campus. In general, all divisions of continuing adult education are not receiving adequate support. The Dean of University College is responsible to the President of the University. Audio-visual aids are available for instruction.

VII. Student Recruitment

Some newspaper and radio publicity are used.

* * *

St. Bonaventure University
St. Bonaventure, N. Y.
Evening Session

Total enrollment 2,565   Private Church-related
Evening enrollment 444   University
                                    Semester System

I. Admission Policies

The deadline for application for admission to evening classes is three days prior to the first class. A student may register conditionally for credit courses before transcripts are submitted. "Special" students working for certification may take sufficient courses for credit to qualify for a certificate. "Special" students at St. Bonaventure University are those students who have degrees and are seeking certification to teach. They must furnish transcripts for admission purposes. Regular students also submit transcripts, but no ACT or CEEB scores are required. Mail registration is used. The students mail course selections to the Computer Section. On registration day, he pays his tuition and fees, and is given his schedule. New students do not register by mail. The Admissions Office formulates the admission policies for the evening students. Few day students take evening classes unless necessary; few evening students take day courses, but there is no rule against mixing day and evening students in the same class. No Orientation program is held for evening students.

II. Terminology

Title of Division: Evening Session. Defined: This covers classes taught in the evening. These are scheduled apart from those taught from 8:00 a. m. to 3:00 p. m. Definition of Continuing Education: "We tend to think of it as an opportunity for adults to work for a degree, or to become certified in education."

III. Fees

There is a fee differential between day and evening classes. Evening courses are paid for by the hour, and day students pay a flat fee for tuition.

IV. Faculty and Faculty Recruitment

98% of the faculty teaching evening classes are full-time. No full-time faculty members teach exclusively in the evening. The Vice-President for Academic Affairs has the final authority for hiring full and part-time faculty members for evening classes. Faculty members may teach credit and non-credit courses as an overload "with limits which do not impair his effectiveness."

V. Scheduling

The Director of the Evening Session is responsible for the evening class schedule. The evening class schedule comes to the Director through the Deans and the Registrar, and the Director schedules the rooms and the hours. Three-

St. Bonaventure University (cont.)

hour classes are scheduled either one or two nights per week depending on the subject. Day and evening classes are equal in quality. Part-time evening students are not eligible for the Dean's List.

VI. General

There is very little opportunity at the present time for students to participate in discussions on the academic program. In general, adequate stress and financial support is given to the evening program by the administration. The Director of the Evening Session is responsible to the Vice-President for Academic Affairs.

VII. Student Recruitment

News stories and advertisements are used for publicity purposes together with spot announcements on the radio. Little use is made of television. Limited contact is made with industry.

* * *

St. Francis College
Brooklyn, N.Y.
Evening Sessions

Total enrollment 2,353   Church-related Institu-
Evening enrollment 321   tion
Semester System

I. Admission Policies

There is no deadline for application for admission to evening classes. Students may not register for credit courses before transcripts are submitted. There is no "special" student category. Admission requirements for regular students is a high school diploma with 16 units. No ACT or CEEB scores are required for admission. Mail registration is used. Students pre-register with an advisor and mail in their registration. At registration period only course changes are made. These changes must be approved by the advisor. Retention policy: a student may be continued on probation one time, and if a 1.75 GPA for a sophomore or a 2.00 average is not obtained, a student is dropped (on a

4. 0 basis). St. Francis College is considering offering a special degree program for adults. The Faculty Committee on Admissions formulates the admission policies for evening students. Students may enroll in both day and evening classes. An Orientation program for evening students is held during registration.

II. Terminology

Title of Division: Evening Sessions. Defined: As opposed to Day Sessions. Definition of Continuing Education: Education beyond the Secondary Level without degree designation.

III. Fees

There is no fee differential between day and evening classes in tuition. However, students in the Evening Session pay $10 college fee; day students pay a $35 college fee. Refund policy: full refund before the end of the first week. After that time, no refund.

IV. Faculty and Faculty Recruitment

Approximately 75% of the faculty teaching evening classes are full-time. No full-time faculty members teach exclusively in the evening. The Board of Trustees has the final authority for hiring full- and part-time faculty. No faculty meetings are held for evening faculty. Overloads for faculty members are discouraged.

V. Scheduling

The Director of Evening Sessions has the responsibility for the evening class schedule. Three-hour classes are held two nights a week. Day and evening classes are equal in quality. Part-time evening students are eligible for the Dean's List by taking eight or more hours with a 3. 0 average.

VI. General

Students participate in discussions regarding the academic program through their Student Government which is an

St. Francis College (cont.)

Academic Affairs Committee. The Academic Dean meets with student leaders four times a year. Adequate stress and financial support is given to the Evening Session. The Director of Evening Session is responsible to the Academic Dean.

VII. Student Recruitment

Newspaper stories and advertisements are used for publicity purposes.

* * *

St. Joseph's College
Evening College
Philadelphia, Pennsylvania

Total enrollment 6, 600
Evening enrollment 4, 800

Private, Church-related
Institution
Semester System

I. Admission Policies

Deadline for application is 30 days prior to term beginning. Students may register for credit courses without transcripts. "Isolated Credit" status permits students to take courses on a non-degree basis but matriculation is encouraged. Admission requirements: High school graduation. Mail registration is used. (Last fall 30% pre-registered.) Students must maintain 1.5 for 18 credits; 1.7--30 credits; 1.9--60 credits; 2.0 required for graduation. No special degree program is offered and not considered. Admission policies are set by the Dean and his staff. (New College Council has Standards Committee.) Day and Evening students may enroll in the same class with permission of their deans. There is an orientation program for evening students on Saturday or Sunday afternoon before term begins.

II. Terminology

Title of Division: Recently changed from Evening Division to Evening College. Continuing Education, defined: Courses for B. A. and B. S. Graduates to keep up to date, etc.

III. Fees

Day students pay by the year or semester. Everyone's fees are assessed by the course. Refund policy: 40%--first week; 20%--second week through 5th week; 6th week--0%.

IV. Faculty and Faculty Recruitment

38% teaching evening classes are full-time. Final authority to hire evening faculty lies with the Dean with validation by the President. Some full-time faculty members teach exclusively in the evening. Faculty meetings are held annually with everyone; departments meet several times a year. Non-credit courses are taught by regular faculty; institutes, etc. are not handled by this division.

V. Scheduling

The Dean is responsible for the schedule. Three credit hour classes are scheduled two nights a week and only rarely once a week. Research: There is a continuing study on Admissions (since 1964) in order to determine whether high school graduates or adults make better students; results indicate those out of high school for a number of years earn better grades. Students are eligible for the Dean's List, Evening College, after completing 30 hours with a "B."

VI. General

There has been a student council for evening students in operation for ten years. The evening division is receiving adequate support. The Dean of the Evening Division is responsible to the Executive Vice-President. Audio-visual aids are available.

VII. Student Recruitment

Newspaper (10 papers--3 ads a yr.) and radio publicity are used. Public relations: descriptive brochures are sent out.

* * *

St. Louis University
Metropolitan College
St. Louis, Mo.

Total enrollment 10,000   Private, church-related
Evening enrollment 2,000   institution
                                     Semester system

I. Admission Policies

The deadline for application for admission to evening
classes is the day of registration. Students may register for
credit courses before transcripts are submitted. Non-matriculating or "special" students may take an unlimited number of courses for credit. Scores on ACT or CEEB are not
necessarily required for admission but may be used if necessary for advisement. A special degree program for adults
is being considered for adoption. Mail registration is used
for Metropolitan College non-degree credit courses only. The
various colleges formulate the admission policies for evening
students. Day and evening students may enroll in the same
class. An Orientation program is held for evening students
at the beginning of each semester.

II. Terminology

Title of Division: Metropolitan College (degree programs are administered by the evening division of the College
of Arts or the School of Commerce and Finance). Definition
of Metropolitan College: Continuing, non-degree education
for adults. Definition of Continuing Education: The learning
needed for a satisfying life, that can be accomplished only
after completion of each individual's formal education.

III. Fees

There is a fee differential for students attending day
or evening classes. Day students pay $53 per sem. hr.;
evening students pay $37 per sem. hr. This is due to fewer
services offered evening students. Students receive refunds
for courses dropped on a percentage scale through 1/2 of the
semester.

210

IV. Faculty and Faculty Recruitment

85% of the faculty teaching evening classes in Metropolitan College are full-time. None in the evening division of Arts and Sciences or Commerce and Finance are fulltime. The Deans of the various schools are responsible for hiring full- or part-time faculty members for evening classes. No faculty meetings are held for evening faculty. Faculty members are paid for teaching overloads in the evening.

V. Scheduling

The Dean of Metropolitan College is responsible for the evening class schedule in his own college. The Dean of Arts and Sciences and Commerce and Finance are responsible for their respective programs. The registrar collects and publishes information regarding the evening class schedule. The evening classes in Metropolitan College compare favorably with the day classes. However, those classes offered by other colleges may not be on quite the same level as day classes. Part-time evening students are eligible for the Dean's List.

VI. General

Students do not have an opportunity to participate in discussions regarding the academic program. In general, more support could be given to the evening program. The need and importance of adult education is generally not understood by the administration. The Dean of Metropolitan College is responsible to the Academic Vice-President.

VII. Student Recruitment

Publicity includes ads and news releases in the newspaper, and spot announcements on radio and television. Special programs are developed for business and industry and for civic organizations.

* * *

Sir George Williams University
Evening Division
Montreal, Canada

Total enrollment 18,726   Private Institution
Evening enrollment 12,062   Semester System

211

Sir George Williams University (cont.)

I. Admission Policies

Deadline for application for admission to evening classes is about two months prior to registration. Students may not register for credit courses without submitting transcripts. Admission requirements are the same as for day students unless a person wants to enter under "mature matriculation" status. Students enrolled in evening classes must maintain the same academic standards as all day students. There is no special degree for adults. Admission policies for all students are set by the University Council. Day students are allowed to enroll in evening classes but not viceversa. There is no orientation program for evening students.

II. Terminology

Title of Division: Evening Division, defined: Includes all classes scheduled after 6:00 p.m. and Saturday mornings. All education is, or ought to be, continuing education, i.e., related to what has gone on in the past and oriented toward the possibilities of the future.

III. Fees

There is no fee differential between day and evening classes. 25% refunds are made if drops are within the first two weeks of class; no refunds are made after that.

IV. Faculty and Faculty Recruitment

Final authority to hire faculty lies with academic deans with recommendations from department chairmen.

V. Scheduling

The Registrar is responsible for the class schedules in consultation with the academic deans. Three credit hour courses are scheduled one night a week. There is no significant difference in grade distribution between day and evening classes. Part-time evening students are eligible for the Dean's List after completing 30 semester hours with a 3.0 grade point average.

VI. General

Students participate in discussions regarding academic programs by holding membership on all important councils and boards, including the University Council and Academic Planning Committee. The evening division is receiving adequate support. Complete audio-visual instructional aids are available for use in evening classes.

VII. Student Recruitment

The annual calendar and time table of courses are distributed to students.

* * *

University of Southern California
Los Angeles, Cal.
University College

Total enrollment 18,000   Private Institution
Evening enrollment 5,000   Semester System

I. Admission Policies

There is no deadline for application for admission to evening classes. Students may register for credit courses before transcripts are submitted. "Special" students may take a maximum of three graduate courses or four undergraduate courses before matriculation. The admission requirements for "special" students is high school graduation or 21 years of age; for regular students high school graduation and CEEB and GRE scores. A special degree program for adults is being considered for possible adoption at the university. The Admissions Committee formulates the admission policies for the evening students. There is a great overlapping of day students in evening classes--there are no restrictions. No Orientation Program is held for evening students.

II. Terminology

Title of Division: University College. Defined: As presently constituted, it is more of an "extended day" operation to assist regular degree-bound students than something especially tailored for "special" students. It also includes extension courses, credit and non-credit. Definition of Con-

213

University of Southern California (cont.)

tinuing Education: Broadly to include both credit and non-credit programs--both regular and special degree programs offered both on and off campus--day or evening for persons who have previously completed a course of study.

III. Fees

There is no fee differential between day and evening classes. The refund policies for evening students are the same as for day students.

IV. Faculty and Faculty Recruitment

Approximately 60% of the faculty members teaching evening classes are full-time. No full-time faculty members teach exclusively in the evening. The academic department chairman or dean of the appropriate academic school or college has the final authority for hiring full- and part-time faculty members for evening classes. No regular faculty meetings are held for evening faculty, but they are invited to attend departmental faculty meetings. Faculty members may teach credit or non-credit courses as an overload--but the normal limit is one credit course "overload" each semester.

V. Scheduling

The Assistant Dean of University College is responsible for the evening class schedule together with the Academic Vice-President's office which is concerned with the total University schedule. The course and professor lists are submitted to University College for inclusion in the program. Three-hour classes are scheduled either one night or two nights a week. The university envisions some studies on the use of TV in achieving economy efficiency related goals and in teacher education and in extending off-campus "in-plant." Comparing day and evening classes in terms of quality there is "no real difference--only sometimes psychological attitudinal factors result in reduction in rigor of evening classes. In many cases, the evening class is academically superior to the day class." Part-time evening students are eligible for the Dean's List with requirements varying with the different schools.

VI.   General

Credit and non-credit courses in off-campus locations for economically deprived populations include special tutorial projects, Social Action Institute, Urban semester programs and a Medical program in Watts. Students are participating in discussions regarding the academic program to a growing extent. Student representatives now sit as regular members of most all University committees. Innovative practices used: Intersession Summer Program--June 10-July 10; Black history and sociology programs taught by Negro scholars; projected degree programs for adults; projected cooperation with independent continuing education projects in Southern California in non-credit liberal arts discussion programs; television education--public relations programs; Excellence in Teaching Awards program; numerous special conferences and institutes; overseas programs for regular students and military persons and dependents; and Alumni Continuing Education Programs. More stress and financial support could be given to the evening program. The Deans of University College report to the Vice-President of Academic Affairs.

VII.   Student Recruitment

General 3-column display ads are placed in the metropolitan press at the beginning of each semester. Some special ads on special programs are sent to newspapers at various times, and a limited number of free public service announcements of the general program and special courses are used on radio. Very little use is made of television for publicity purposes. Special brochures for special programs are sent to business and industry. Specially developed mailing lists are used for civic clubs and organizations including literature for prospective students.

* * *

Southern Connecticut State College
New Haven, Connecticut
Extension Services

Total enrollment 10,400   Public Institution
Evening enrollment 4,700   Semester System

I.   Admission Policies

Deadline for application for evening students is by the first day of classes. Students may register for credit courses

215

Southern Connecticut State College (cont.)

without transcripts on a provisional basis. Non-matriculated students may take a maximum of 30 semester hours. Admission requirements are high school graduation, a "C" average on previous college work or satisfactory CEEB scores. Mail registration is open to matriculated students only. Matriculated students must maintain a "C" average. There is no special degree for adults. Admission policies are set by the Admissions Committee. Day and evening students may register in the same classes with permission. There is no orientation for evening students.

II. Terminology

Title of Division: Extension Services, defined: Evening Division, including all programs: graduate, undergraduate and special after end of regular day courses.

III. Fees

Evening students pay $30.00 for graduate courses per semester hour and $25.00 per semester hour for undergraduate courses; day students pay $100 annually. This is justified because day classes are state subsidized. Refunds are made because of illness--1/2 of total tuition; because of being drafted--total.

IV. Faculty and Faculty Recruitment

50% teaching evening classes are full-time. Final authority to hire evening faculty lies with the President. The Director of Extension Services may reject a faculty member assigned to teach evening classes. No regular faculty meetings are held. Overloads for faculty members are not permitted.

V. Scheduling

The Director is responsible for the evening class schedule. Three credit hour classes are scheduled two nights a week. Day and evening classes are equal in terms of quality. Part-time evening students are not eligible for the Dean's List.

VI. General

In general, all evening divisions are not receiving adequate support. The Director of Extension Services is responsible to the President. Audio-visual instructional aids are available for evening classes.

VII. Student Recruitment

Newspaper, radio and television publicity are used. Special motivational appeals have been developed for industry and civic organizations.

* * *

University of Southern Mississippi
Hattiesburg, Mississippi
Division of Continuing Education

Total enrollment 8, 000   Public Institution
Evening enrollment 1, 500   Quarter System

I. Admission Policies

Deadline for application for admission for regular students is three weeks prior to registration; there is no deadline for non-degree students. Students may take a maximum of 16 quarter hours as non-matriculating students. Admission requirements are high school graduation or recommendation from last college attended. The ACT examination is required for adults in the evening division and is used as a basis for admission as well as for advisement. There is no special degree program for adults but one is being considered. Admission policies are set by the Academic Council. Day and evening students may enroll in the same classes. Orientation for evening students is combined with day students' orientation.

II. Terminology

Title of Division: Division of Continuing Education defined: The administrative unit responsible for all credit and non-credit programs over and above those administered by day deans of the university.

University of Southern Mississippi (cont.)

III. Fees

Refunds are made to students on a graduated percentage basis.

IV. Faculty and Faculty Recruitment

A ratio of 50-50 is maintained regarding the percentage of faculty teaching evening classes. Final authority to hire evening faculty lies with the Board of Trustees of Institutions of Higher Learning of the State of Mississippi. The Dean of the Division of Continuing Education can reject a faculty member assigned to teach evening classes. Some full-time faculty members teach exclusively in the evening; they are responsible to the Dean of the Division. Regular faculty meetings are held the second week of the quarter. Faculty members are not allowed to teach on an overload basis.

V. Scheduling

The Dean of the Division of Continuing Education is not responsible for the evening class schedule. The Academic Deans are. The Dean of the Division of Continuing Education may not revise or make additions to the evening class schedule. Three credit hour courses are scheduled one night a week. Day and evening classes are equal in terms of quality. Part-time evening students are eligible for the Dean's List with a grade point average of 3.25 after completing 15 quarter hours.

VI. General

Students participate very little in discussions regarding academic programs. In general, all evening divisions are not receiving adequate support. The Dean of the Division of Continuing Education is responsible to the Dean of the University. Audio-visual instructional aids are available for evening classes.

VII. Student Recruitment

Newspaper and radio publicity are used. Sometimes

218

guest speakers are included in programs for the Chamber of Commerce and other civic organizations.

* * *

Springfield College
Springfield, Mass.
Division of Continuing Education
Total enrollment 1, 900   Private Institution
Evening enrollment 400   Semester System

I. Admission Policies

The deadline for application for admission to evening classes for freshmen is February 15. For non-degree students there is no deadline. Students may register for credit courses before transcripts are submitted. "Special" or non-degree students may take as many as 30 semester hours work for credit. The admission requirement for "special" students includes a high school diploma; for regular students, a Scholastic Aptitude Test is required, together with an English Composition Achievement Test with no cutoff point plus all regular credentials--transcripts, medical examination and recommendations. Mail registration will go into effect by the summer of 1969. Retention policies: 1. 70 freshmen; 1. 85--sophomores; 1. 95--juniors; 2. 00--seniors. No special retention policies for "special students. The Director of Continuing Education in conjunction with the Committee on Admissions formulates the admission policies for evening students. The Director of the Division of Continuing Education formulates policies for "special" students. Day and evening students may enroll in the same class if day students have class conflicts or schedule problems. An Orientation Program for evening students is held in September.

II. Terminology

Title of Division: Division of Continuing Education. Defined: Continuing Education basically represents the opportunity for adults to earn their undergraduate degree on a part-time basis. It also includes non-credit institutes, conferences, workshops and extension courses.

III. Fees

There is no fee differential for day and evening classes.

219

Springfield College (cont.)

Refund policies: full reimbursement up to the end of the third week of class. After the beginning of the fourth week, there is no reimbursement.

IV. Faculty and Faculty Recruitment

Approximately 75% of the faculty teaching evening classes are full-time, and full-time faculty members have priority in teaching during the evening. The Director of the Division of Continuing Education has the final authority for hiring full and part-time faculty members for evening classes. No regular faculty meetings are held for evening faculty. Full-time faculty can teach one course each ten-week term as an overload. Total participation for additional responsibilities including non-credit institutes should not exceed 120%.

V. Scheduling

The Director of the Division of Continuing Education is responsible for the evening class schedule. Recommendations are made by the Division Heads, with the final scheduling made by the Committee on Continuing Education with the approval of the Director. Three-hour classes are held one or two nights per week. Many four-hour classes are now scheduled for two evenings. Day and evening classes compare favorably in quality. Part-time evening students are not eligible for the Dean's List.

VI. General

Students participate on the Student Advisory Board and have representation on the Committee on Continuing Education: The decision and policy making committee for Continuing Education. Open House Workshops are held for library administrators. Some day classes are designed for adults. More stress and financial support should be given to the evening program. The Director of Continuing Education is responsible to the Academic Dean.

VII. Student Recruitment

Newspaper advertisements and stories are used for

publicity purposes together with spot announcements on the radio. Little use is made of television. Non-credit management seminars are held for business and industry.

* * *

Suffolk University
Boston, Mass.
Evening Division

Total enrollment 4, 058   Private Institution
Evening enrollment 892   Semester System
(plus 708 evening law students)

I. Admission Policies

Deadlines for regular students: Sept. 17, January 22 and June 16. Deadlines for "special" students: September 25, February 10, and June 19. Students may register for credit courses before transcripts are submitted if they are "special" students or if credit is to be transferred to another college. At least 30 hours may be taken for credit as a "special" student, with some additional hours allowed with special permission. Admission requirements for "special" students includes high school graduation with no SAT - CEEB required for "older" students. Admission requirements for regular students includes high school graduation, SAT - CEEB (waived for mature students). Transfer students must have a 2. 0 (C) average. Mail registration is used for day and evening summer students. Students submit course selections and check to the Accounting Office. The Accounting Office refers course selections form to the Registrar who mails registration forms and class slips to the student. Retention policies: 1. 8--freshmen; 1. 9--sophomores; 2. 0--juniors and seniors. Sometimes C. L. E. P. or reading tests are required. The Bachelor of Sciences in General Studies is offered as a special degree program for adults--with 29 students enrolled in the program. A revision of the program is being considered. The Director of the Evening Division together with the Faculty Admissions Committee and Director of Admissions formulates the admission policies for evening students. Day and evening classes are interchangeable, but first year evening students may not normally take day courses. No Orientation program for evening students is held, but an Orientation program may be held next year.

II. Terminology

Title of Division: Evening Division. Defined: It is

221

Suffolk University (cont.)

responsible for graduate and undergraduate evening courses
(with the exception of Law which is a separate unit), and for
extension courses. We offer no non-credit courses at present, but could if we had the staff and space. Definition of
Continuing Education: "I tend to associate Adult Education
with non-credit courses, and Continuing Education with credit
courses. "

III. Fees

Tuition is $40 per semester hour for both full-time
day students and evening with the exception that full-time day
students pay $1200 per year. Refund policies: 80%--within
1st week; 60% within 2nd week; 40% within 3rd week; 20%
within 4th week; thereafter--0.

IV.   Faculty and Faculty Recruitment

70% of the faculty teaching evening classes are full-
time. All full-time faculty are required to teach evening
courses as part of their full teaching load when they are
needed. The President and the Board of Trustees have the
final authority for hiring full- and part-time faculty. No
faculty meetings are held for evening faculty. Faculty members may teach extension courses, or institutes for extra
pay, but may not teach regular courses as an overload at our
institution.

V. Scheduling

The Associate Dean of the Evening Division has the
responsibility for the evening class schedule together with the
day deans and department chairmen. The registrar assigns
classrooms. Department chairmen recommend course offerings and teaching assignments. These are modified in order
to provide a balanced schedule and to minimize course conflicts. Three-hour courses are scheduled one or two nights
a week. The Associate Dean of the Evening Division is co-
ordinating a Long-Range Study that includes both day and evening divisions. Day and evening classes are equal in quality.
Part-time evening students are eligible for the Dean's List
by taking 9 sem. hrs. with a 3. 0 (B) average.

VI. General

Scholarship assistance is available to economically deprived individuals who are qualified to take college work. Students participate in discussions regarding the academic program through a Joint Student-Faculty Committee. Recommendations are made by student government. Suffolk University has an Interdisciplinary Senior Honors Program; also students are placed in Social Work Agencies as part of their Field Experience course. Adequate stress and financial support is given to the evening program. The Dean is responsible directly to the Vice-President and Dean of the College of Liberal Arts and Sciences.

VII. Student Recruitment

Newspaper stories and ads are used for publicity. No use of radio and television is made for publicity purposes. Special announcements are prepared for business and industry and for civic organizations.

* * *

Syracuse University
University College

Total enrollment 23,000   Private Institution
Evening enrollment 6,000   Semester System

I. Admission Policies

There is no deadline for application for admission to evening classes and students may register for credit courses before transcripts are received. Students may take up to 9 hours at graduate level, as non-matriculating students; no limit for undergraduate courses. Admission requirements are high school graduation, transcripts, letters of recommendation, and College Board Exams. Mail registration is only used for non-credit courses. Students must maintain a "C" average in order to remain in college. A special degree program for adults is offered: Bachelor of Arts (Liberal Studies). The Admissions Office formulates the admission policies for the evening students; for special students: University College with Faculty Committee.

223

II. Terminology

Title of Division: University College, defined: It is the Continuing Education Division of the University. Continuing Education: Credit courses, day and evening, non-credit courses, conferences, institutes, etc. , which focus on the part-time and adult student.

III. Fees

Refunds are made through first five weeks of classes and none thereafter.

IV. Faculty and Faculty Recruitment

95% teaching evening classes are full-time faculty members. Final authority to hire faculty lies with University College in consultation with Deans and Department Chairmen. Faculty members are allowed no more than one overload a semester. Non-credit courses are not included.

V. Scheduling

The Dean of University College is responsible for the schedule of evening classes. 3 credit hour classes are scheduled either one or two nights per week. Research: (Staff members are about to do doctoral dissertations on attitudes of faculty toward Continuing Education Division.) Part-time students not eligible for the Dean's List.

VI. General

Special courses are offered in the ghetto at appropriate locations. In general, evening divisions are not receiving adequate support. The Dean of the Evening Division is responsible to the Vice-President for Continuing Education and through him to Vice-President for Academic Affairs. Audio-visual aids are used extensively.

VII. Student Recruitment

Newspaper, radio and television publicity are used. Public relations: special motivational appeals have been developed for industry and organizations, personal contacts, phone campaigns, magazines, etc.

* * *

University of Tampa
Continuing Education
Tampa, Florida

Total enrollment 1, 978   Private Institution
Evening enrollment 400   Semester System

I. Admission Policies

There is a deadline for application for admission to evening classes which is the starting date for each semester. Students may register without transcripts with permission from the Director of Admissions. Non-matriculated students may take 12 semester hours work which is validated by performance. Admission requirements are high school graduation or GED and scores on CEEB tests (for regular degree students). A special degree program for adults is being considered. Admission policies are set by the Director of Admissions. Day and evening students may enroll in the same classes. There is no orientation for evening students.

II. Terminology

Title of Division: Continuing Education. Defined: Offers courses for credit or non-credit (as the student qualifies, or if the material is of college level. Courses open with above restrictions to all community).

III. Fees

There is no fee differential for day and evening classes for credit. Students are charged drop fee of $3.00 and obtain full refund if change is made before classes start. Otherwise sliding scale refunds are made.

University of Tampa (cont.)

IV. Faculty and Faculty Recruitment

25% teaching evening classes are full-time faculty members. Final authority to hire faculty members lies with the Vice-President for Academic Affairs. The Director of Continuing Education can reject a faculty member assigned to teach evening classes. No regular faculty meetings are held. Faculty members are paid extra if they teach on an overload basis.

V. Scheduling

The Director of Continuing Education is responsible for the evening class schedule in consultation with the Registrar and Department heads. Three-credit hour classes are scheduled both one and two nights a week depending on the course. Day and evening classes are equal in terms of quality but at some times the evening courses suffer due to part-time faculty. Part-time evening students are not eligible for the Dean's List.

VI. General

Students are members of many committees and participate in discussions regarding academic programs through them. Committee participation is being expanded, plus weekly open meetings with the President, Vice President and Department Chairmen. The Director of Continuing Education is responsible to the Vice President for Academic Affairs.

VII. Student Recruitment

Newspaper, radio and television publicity are used. Special motivational appeals have been developed for industry and civic organizations such as the Chamber of Commerce.

* * *

University of Tennessee
Division of University Extension
Knoxville, Tennessee

Total enrollment 30,000	Public Institution
Evening enrollment 6,000	Quarter System
(in three centers)	

I. Admission Policies

There is no deadline for application for admission to evening classes and students may register for credit courses without submitting transcripts. Non-matriculated students may take a maximum of 90 quarter hours before entering a degree program. Admission requirements are 21 years of age or high school diploma; regular students must have a high school average of 2. 25 or better and ACT scores. Students must maintain 1. 5 after 36 quarter hours, 2. 0 after 84 quarter hours. A special degree for adults is being considered. Admission policies are set by the Faculty Senate. Day and evening students may register in the same classes. There is no orientation for evening students.

II. Terminology

Title of Division: Division of University Extension. Defined: Extension of University credit programs plus service to communities in the state. Continuing Education is any organized educational program, credit courses given primarily to adults; non-credit courses, conferences and institutes.

III. Fees

There is no fee differential between day and evening classes. Refund policy: Cost to student for drop prior to beginning of classes--$10; through end of first week of classes--$15; through end of second week of classes--$20. Drop after second week of classes--no refund.

IV. Faculty and Faculty Recruitment

50-75% teaching evening classes are full-time faculty members; this policy is required by the Accrediting Association for the Day Division. Final authority to hire faculty lies with the academic department chairmen. The Dean of the Division of University Extension can reject a faculty member assigned to teach evening classes. Some full-time faculty members are employed exclusively in the evening and are responsible to the Director of the Division of University Extension. Regular faculty meetings are held each fall. Faculty members are permitted to teach one credit class per quarter on an overload basis.

227

University of Tennessee (cont.)

V. Scheduling

The Dean of University Extension is responsible for the evening class schedule, and has the authority to revise it. Three-credit hour courses are scheduled both one and two nights a week depending on staff and content. Day and evening classes are equal in terms of quality and sometimes particular classes are better. Part-time evening students are eligible for the Dean's List with 12 quarter hours and a 3.0 or better.

VI. General

Students participate in discussion regarding academic program very little. Special mini-grants up to $200 are available to any instructor who has some teaching innovation he wants to try. The evening division is not receiving adequate stress but the situation is improving. The Dean of the Division of University Extension is responsible to the Vice-Chancellor for Academic Affairs. Audio-visual instructional aids are available for evening classes.

VII. Student Recruitment

Newspaper publicity is used for recruiting students. Special motivational appeals have been developed for industry and various organizations.

* * *

Texas Christian University
Evening Division
Fort Worth, Texas

Total enrollment 6,500   Church-related Institution
Evening enrollment 1,500   Semester System

I. Admission Policies

If admission procedures are not completed at the time of registration, students are admitted provisionally. There is no limit to the amount of work a student may take as a non-matriculating student. Mail registration is used: Students request mail registration kit, complete it and return it, the staff processes the registration before regular registra-

228

tion. Students must maintain a "C" average. A special degree program for adults is offered: Bachelor of Arts degree with divisional concentration in Humanities, Natural Sciences (including math) or Social Sciences, Admission policies are set by the Admissions Office in consultation with Evening College and University Council. Day and evening students may enroll in the same class.

II. Terminology

Title of Division: The Evening College, defined: An extension of the University facilities into the evening hours in order to make university education available to those unable to attend classes in the day and especially to fix responsibility for seeing that the needs of adults are met.

III. Fees

Tuition is charged until the date of official withdrawal according to a set table: 1 week or less: 10%; 2 weeks: 20%; 3 weeks: 30%; 4 weeks: 50%; 5 weeks: 70%; 6 weeks 90%; over 6 weeks: 100%.

IV. Faculty and Faculty Recruitment

The policy regarding the percentage of faculty for evening classes that are full time is a minimum of 25%; approximately 40% are full time. Final authority for hiring faculty lies with Dean and department chairmen jointly. Some full-time faculty members teach exclusively in the evening. Regular faculty meetings are held annually for entire faculty and periodically for groups. Faculty may teach only non-credit courses on an overload basis.

V. Scheduling

The Dean of the Evening College is responsible for the schedule. Three credit hour classes are scheduled either one or two nights per week. Part-time students are not eligible for the Dean's List.

229

Texas Christian University (cont.)

VI. General

The students participate in discussion regarding academic programs through the Student Council. Special seminars are held for faculty membrs in order to increase teaching effectiveness. The Dean is responsible to the Vice-Chancellor.

VII. Student Recruitment

Newspaper, radio and television publicity are used. Public relations: special motivational appeals have been developed for industry and organizations. A joint effort with SMU and the University of Dallas is being made to offer courses to six industrial plants via television.

* * *

Thomas More College
Saturday and Evening Division
Covington, Kentucky

Total enrollment 3,030   Church-related Institu-
Evening enrollment 953 credit,   tion
    873 non-credit   Semester System

I. Admission Policies

Deadline for admission to evening classes is two weeks after classes begin. Students may register for credit courses without transcripts. There is no limit to the number of hours of credit work a non-matriculated student may take. Admission requirement is high school graduation. Students must maintain a 2.0 cumulative after 30 hours if they did not meet admission standards of the Day Division and 2.0 after 64 hours if they did meet the admissions standards of the day division. Admission policies are set by the Director of the Evening and Saturday Division in conjunction with the Admissions Committee. Day and evening students may register in the same classes. There is no orientation program for evening students.

II. Terminology

Title of Division: Evening and Saturday Division.

Continuing Education, defined: All work taken on a part-time basis for self improvement or cultural development.

III. Fees

Day and evening tuition is $26 a credit hour. Refunds: 100% first week, 80% second week, 60% third week, 40% fourth week, 20% fifth week, 0% thereafter.

IV. Faculty and Faculty Recruitment

33% teaching evening classes are full-time faculty members. Final authority to hire faculty lies with the President. The Director of the Evening and Saturday Division may reject a faculty member asssigned to teach evening classes. No regular faculty meetings are held. Overloads for faculty members are permitted if the Academic Dean approves them.

V. Scheduling

The Director of Evening and Saturday Classes is responsible for the evening class schedule, and has the authority to revise it. Three-credit hour courses are scheduled one night a week. Day and evening classes are equal in terms of quality, possibly slightly inferior in Literature and Philosophy, somewhat higher in Business Administration. Part-time evening students are eligible for the Dean's List with a minimum of 8 credit hours and a GPA of 3.5.

VI. General

Non-credit courses are offered in converted Elementary schools in urban areas. Students discuss academic programs through extensive counseling. Non-credit students are surveyed for courses of possible interest. The evening division is receiving adequate stress and financial support, but the faculty does not completely recognize the importance of continuing education. The Director of Evening and Saturday Division is responsible to the Academic Dean. Audio-visual instructional aids are available for evening classes.

Thomas More College (cont.)

VII.   Student Recruitment

Newspaper publicity is used.   Special motivational appeals have been developed for industry in the form of individual letters to Personnel Directors each semester.   Letters
are also sent to Directors of Civic Organizations each semester and various clubs are on the mailing lists.

* * *

University of Toledo
Toledo, Ohio
Division of Adult Continuing Education

Total enrollment 13, 000   Public Institution
Evening enrollment 4, 000   Quarter System

I.   Admission Policies

Deadline for application for admission to evening
classes is one month prior to the registration date.   Students
may not register for credit courses before transcripts are
submitted.   Students do not register as "special" students.
Admission requirements for regular students: they must submit high school and/or college transcripts.   Beginning students are expected to submit scores on the CEEB.   Mail
registration is used.   Students obtain approved programs for
registration; the registrar handles registration.   Bills are
sent out and they must be paid before the previous quarter
ends.   3/4 of the students register by mail.   There is no
retention policy for evening students.   CEEB Placement tests
are used.   No special degree program is offered for adults.
The Faculty Admissions Committee together with the Admissions Office formulates the admission policies for evening
students.   Day and evening students may enroll in the same
classes.   No orientation program is scheduled for evening
students.

II.   Terminology

Title of Division: Division of Adult Continuing Education.   Defined: The Division of Adult and Continuing Education operates as a part of the year-round service of the University, providing degree work through the various colleges,
as well as instruction for groups interested in non-credit
special programs.   Responsibility for coordination of this

program rests upon this division, but credit courses whether offered during the day or evening are the responsibility of the Dean of the College insofar as content, faculty, academic regulations and standards are concerned. Continuing Education is all phases of study-credit, non-credit, conferences, institutes for remedial retreading, updating.

III. Fees

There is no fee differential between day and evening classes. Refund policy: Before the first day of classes-- 100%; on the first eight calendar days--90%; on the fourteenth calendar day--60%. In non-credit courses there is no refund after the class convenes.

IV. Faculty and Faculty Recruitment

Nearly all faculty members teaching evening classes are full-time. No full-time faculty members teach exclusively in the evening. The academic deans have the final authority for hiring full- and part-time faculty. Department heads must staff classes. Regular faculty members receive additional compensation for teaching non-credit courses, institutes and conferences as an overload.

V. Scheduling

The academic deans are responsible for the evening class schedule, and submit the schedule to the registrar. Three-hour classes are scheduled two evenings per week. Day and evening classes are equal in quality. Part-time evening students are not eligible for the Dean's List.

VI. General

Students participate in discussions regarding the academic program through student government. Honors students may participate in non-credit courses for enrichment. Adequate stress and financial support is given to the evening program. The Dean is responsible to the President.

University of Toledo (cont.)

VII. Student Recruitment

The Sunday supplement to the newspaper is used for
publicity purposes together with spot announcements on the
radio. The local educational television station will be used
for publicity stories and announcements this year. The institution mails out 200,000 pieces of promotional literature each
year to business and industry and provides brochures and
Sunday supplements to the Chamber of Commerce.

* * *

University of Toronto
Toronto, Canada
Division of University Extension
Total enrollment 23,000   Public Institution
Quarter System

I. Admission Policies

The deadline for application for admission to evening
classes: August 15 (fall and winter); April 1st (summer evening); May 15th (summer day). Students may not register
for credit courses before transcripts are submitted. There
are no "special" students. Evening students must meet the
same admission requirements as day students, but no ACT or
CEEB scores are required for admission. An English Language
Facility Test is administered when indicated. Mail registration is used: application and registration forms are mailed
to undergraduates and as requested from new students. Before beginning classes, a student is required to consult a
counselor. The following degrees are available to part-time
students: B. A. , B. A. Sc. , B. Sc. , and B. Sc. N. The Committees on Admissions of the faculties concerned formulate
the admission policies for evening students. Day students
may enroll in evening classes by permission and as quota allows in different classes. Evening students receive counselling, library orientation, and enroll in a writing laboratory.

II. Terminology

Title of Division: The Division of University Extension. Defined: Divisions are units of the University as are
colleges, faculties, schools and centers. Continuing Education includes any systematic course of study, credit or non-

234

credit at any level.

III. Fees

There is no fee differential between day and evening classes. A pro-rate refund on each course from which the student withdraws before February 15.

IV. Faculty and Faculty Recruitment

Most of the evening faculty members are full-time, but some are cross-appointed with other faculties or departments. About 90% are full-time. No full-time faculty members teach exclusively in the evening. All the teaching staff are appointed or recommended by the appropriate teaching department. Faculty meetings are held for evening faculty in the late afternoons. Instead of overloads, the institution prefers cross-appointments so that extension programs are part of the faculty member's normal work load. Recruitment of suitable faculty members is the chief obstacle of cross-appointments.

V. Scheduling

The Director is responsible for the evening class schedule. The schedule is compiled by the estimated need based on experience. Schedules are announced six years in advance. Three-hour classes are scheduled either one or two evenings a week. There is no Dean's List.

VI. General

Students participate in discussions regarding the academic program for student members of the curriculum committee--a relatively new feature at the university. More stress and financial support could be given to the evening program. The Director is responsible to the Provost.

VII. Student Recruitment

Newspaper ads and special news stories are used for publicity purposes. Special announcements are made to business and industry. According to the Director, "the chief appeal is to the individual" to meet his needs as he sees them.

* * *

Trenton State College
Trenton, N. J.
Division of Field Services
Total enrollment 9500   Public Institution
Evening enrollment 5200   Semester System

I. Admission Policies

There is no deadline for application for admission to evening classes. A student may register for credit courses before transcripts are submitted. "Special" students may register for credit courses and may take an unlimited number of courses. Admission requirements for all students include high school graduation. No ACT or CEEB scores are required. Students may register for undergraduate courses by mail. The student sends in registration card and a check. In turn, the school sends back the class admit cards and bursar's office receipt. Retention policies: 1.6 after 30 hours attempted, 1.8 after 60 hrs. attempted, and 2.0 after 90 hours. The Dean of Instruction formulates the admission policies in cooperation with the evening director. Day students rarely enroll in the same classes as evening students. No orientation program is held for evening students. An "Open Admission Policy" is used at this institution.

II. Terminology

Title of Division: Division of Field Services. Defined: "The title in no way reflects the function of the division and a title change is forthcoming." Definition of Continuing Education: That work which is undertaken during adult life and may include credit work, non-credit courses and study towards an undergraduate or graduate degree.

III. Fees

Full-time day students pay a flat tuition of $175 per term. Evening undergraduates pay $20 per credit; graduates $25. Refund policies: 100% before classes begin, 60% during first third of term, 30% between first third and first half of term, nothing after the first half of the semester.

IV. Faculty and Faculty Recruitment

Approximately 35% of the faculty for undergraduate courses and 90% of the faculty for graduate courses are full-time faculty members teaching during the evening. No full-time faculty members teach exclusively in the evening. All full-time and part-time faculty members are hired upon the recommendation of department chairmen to the Dean of Instruction. Faculty meetings are held for evening faculty at the beginning of each term. Full-time faculty members are permitted to teach 6 credit hours overload during an academic year.

V. Scheduling

The Director of Field Services is responsible for the evening class schedule. The graduate office gives Field Services the graduate offerings to schedule; the Field Services office determines what undergraduate courses to offer. Three-hour classes are scheduled one evening a week. Day classes are somewhat better in quality than evening classes due to more full-time faculty members. Part-time evening students are not eligible for the Dean's List.

VI. General

Students have no opportunity to participate in any discussions regarding the academic program. More stress and financial support could be given to the evening program-- more emphasis is placed on the day program. The Director of Field Services is responsible to the Dean of Instruction.

VII. Student Recruitment

The institution places advertisements in three local newspapers periodically to publicize special programs.

* * *

The University of Tulsa
Tulsa, Oklahoma
Evening Division

Total enrollment 6, 960   Private, church-related
Evening enrollment 1, 300   Semester System
   (combination day & evening 500)

The University of Tulsa (cont.)

I. Admission Policies

There is no deadline for applications for admission to evening classes. Students may not register for credit classes without a transcript. Transfers must have a 2.0 average. Admission requirements: Submit high school and/or college transcripts, SAT scores (unless student has completed 30 hours). Mail registration is used for enrolling incoming freshmen who because of distance cannot come to the campus to pre-enroll. Retention policy: 2.0 average. The Admissions Committee of the University Council formulates the admission policies for evening students. Day and evening students may enroll in the same class.

II. Terminology

Title of Division: Evening Division. Defined: The Evening Division enrolls students who take all their classes after 6:00 p.m., except Liberal Arts, graduate and Law students. Definition of Continuing Education: Credit courses, advanced degree programs, non-credit courses, conferences and institutes for adults. It also includes cultural activities, discussion groups, etc., sponsored by the Adult Education Council.

III. Fees

Day and evening students pay the same fees. Refund policies: 1st two weeks--80%; 3rd and 4th week--50%; 5th and 6th week--25%; thereafter--0.

IV. Faculty and Faculty Recruitment

Approximately 80-90% of the faculty members teaching evening classes are full time, but no full-time faculty members teach exclusively in the evening. The Dean has the responsibility for hiring full-time and part-time faculty members with the recommendation of the department heads. The final authority lies with the President and Board of Trustees. No faculty meetings are held for evening faculty. Overloads are not permitted except for non-credit courses.

V. Scheduling

The Department heads and the dean are responsible for the class schedule in the evening. Freshmen and sophomore courses are all scheduled two evenings per week; some junior and senior courses meet once per week. Day and evening classes compare favorably in quality. Part-time evening students are eligible for the Dean's List by attaining a "B" average.

VI. General

Students have an opportunity to participate in discussions regarding the academic program through the student senate which sponsors a teacher evaluation questionnaire. The Presidents of all student organizations, senators and other student leaders meet monthly with the President of the University, Dean of Students, the Director of the Evening Division at a dinner meeting and have a discussion of school problems. Adequate support is given to the evening program as a private degree-granting institution. The Director of the Evening Division is responsible to the President.

VII. Student Recruitment

News stories and special announcements are used for publicity, together with some contact made with business and industry. Little use is made of radio and television.

* * *

Virginia Commonwealth University
Richmond, Virginia
The Evening College

Total enrollment 10,600   Public Institution
Evening enrollment 4,000   Semester System
 (plus 4,000 day combination)

I. Admission Policies

Students may be admitted to evening classes: 1. By mail in the month before regular registration. 2. At regular registration. 3. At late registration during the first week of classes. Evening College Special Students: 1. Register for credit classes without submitting a transcript.

Virginia Commonwealth University (cont.)

2. Must submit a form certifying high school graduation and/ or good standing at the previously attended college-level institution. This statement must be certified and mailed by the previous institution. 3. Should take no more than 20 hours of credit before matriculating. <u>Evening College Matriculated Students</u>: 1. Register through Evening College but must be accepted by the specific school involved. 2. ACT or CEEB scores are required for matriculation. Day and evening students may enroll in the same classes. No orientation program is held for evening students.

II. Terminology

Title of Division: The Evening College and the Summer School, with the Director carrying titles as Director of each and the Dean of Continuing Education. Defined: a separate administration, operating much as a second shift would do in industry. Continuing Education defined: Study by adults, either credit or non-credit, in the late afternoon, the evening and on Saturday mornings.

III. Fees

Day and evening students pay the same tuition, but Evening College students do not pay activity fees. Refund policies: prior to beginning of classes--100%; within two weeks (due to illness)--50%. No refund after second week.

IV. Faculty and Faculty Recruitment

Approximately 35% of the faculty teaching evening classes are full-time but no full-time faculty members teach exclusively in the evening. The Deans of the various colleges have the authority for hiring full- and part-time faculty members. Written contracts for adjunct faculty teaching in the Evening College are prepared and signed by the Director. Faculty meetings are held at the beginning of each semester. Faculty members teach evening classes as part of their regular load, but occasionally they are paid for teaching non-credit courses.

V. Scheduling

The Director of the Evening College has the responsibility for scheduling evening classes. The Dean of the particular school originates the academic schedule in cooperation with his Department Chairmen. Most three-hour classes meet one evening per week, with a few classes meeting two evenings. Day and evening classes are equal in terms of quality. Matriculated evening students are eligible for the Dean's List on the same basis as day students.

VI. General

Students have little opportunity to participate in discussion regarding academic programs. Innovative practices used: five classes are taught by educational television; 500-600 adult students attend classes on Saturday mornings. Adequate support is given to the evening program. The Director of the Evening College is responsible to the Vice-President of Academic Affairs and the Provost.

VII. Student Recruitment

The Evening College Catalog is published as a 28-page tabloid-size insert annually. Radio and television publicity is used. Occasional letters are sent to business and industry and to various civic organizations concerning programs.

* * *

Washburn University of Topeka
Topeka, Kan.
Department of Continuing Education
Total enrollment 4,400   Public Institution
Evening enrollment 1,200   Semester System

I. Admission Policies

The deadline for application for admission to evening classes is three weeks before registration. A student may register conditionally for credit courses before transcripts are submitted. "Special" students may take a maximum of 18 sem. hrs. for credit before matriculation. Admission requirements for "special" students include good standing at

Washburn University of Topeka (cont.)

previous institution or out of college at least one year. For regular students, must be a high school graduate, submit ACT scores, and a physical examination for those taking over six hours. No mail registration is used. Retention policies: 1-10 hours--no GPA; 11-32 hrs. --1. 5; 33-54 hrs. --1. 8; over 54 hrs. --2. 0. The Academic Policy Committee formulates the admission policies for evening students. The Director of Admissions sets policies for "special" students. Day and evening students enroll in the same classes. No Orientation program is planned for evening students.

II. Terminology

Title of Division: Department of Continuing Education. Defined: Community service as opposed to classical degree seeking concept applied to other students.

III. Fees

No fee differential is charged for day and evening students. Refund policies: Graduated refund over the first five weeks for withdrawals--partial or total.

IV. Faculty and Faculty Recruitment

Approximately 50% of the faculty teaching evening classes are full-time, but no full-time faculty teach exclusively in the evening. The Director of Continuing Education has the final authority for hiring full- and part-time faculty members for evening classes. A maximum of three credit hours of overload are permitted each semester for faculty members.

V. Scheduling

The Director of Continuing Education is responsible for the evening class schedule, with recommendations of the various departments. Most three-hour classes meet two nights a week; a few meet one night a week. Day and evening classes are approximately equal in quality. Student range of performance is greater than in day classes. Part-time evening students are eligible for the Dean's List by accumulating 12 hours.

VI. General

Students have little opportunity to participate in discussions regarding the academic program. Adequate stress and financial support is given to the evening program. The Director of Continuing Education is responsible to the Vice-President of Academic Affairs.

VII. Student Recruitment

News stories and special announcements are used for publicity purposes, as well as radio and television. Special contacts are made to business and industry and to various civic clubs and organizations.

* * *

Washington University
St. Louis, Missouri
School of Continuing Education

Total enrollment 11,597	Private Institution
Evening enrollment 4,363	Semester System

I. Admission Policies

Deadline for application for admission is prior to the beginning of the second week of courses. Students may register for credit courses without transcripts on a provisional basis. Non-degree students may take a maximum of 60 semester hours. Admission requirements are high school graduation, GED or special examination. Mail registration is used. Mail registrations are accepted up to one week prior to the opening of the semester. Students must maintain a "C" average after completion of 30 hours. Two special degrees for adults are offered: Bachelor of Science and Bachelor of Technology (enrollment 1,000). Admission policies are set by the Administrative Board of the School of Continuing Education and the Summer School. Day and Evening students may register for the same classes with deans' approval.

II. Terminology

Title of Division: School of Continuing Education, defined: includes evening degree and certificate work; also conferences, lectures, and other continuing activities including some professional education.

243

Washington University (cont.)

III. Fees

Day students pay $80 per semester hour, evening students pay $40 per semester hour. This is justified because the cost of instruction for the day is greater.

IV. Faculty and Faculty Recruitment

21% teaching evering classes are full-time. Final authority to hire evening faculty lies with the Dean of the School of Continuing Education. The Dean also has the authority to reject a faculty member if he is unsatisfactory. A faculty member who participates in courses on an overload basis can do so only when the amount received does not exceed 20% of his regular salary.

V. Scheduling

The Dean of the School of Continuing Education is responsible for the evening class schedule. Three credit hour courses are scheduled one night a week, except when laboratories are involved. There is no Dean's List at Washington University.

VI. General

Students participate in discussions regarding the academic program with day faculty and evening administrators in the Committee on Academic Policy. In general, all evening divisions are not receiving adequate support. The Dean is responsible to the Vice Chancellor and Associate Provost. Audio-visual instructional aids are available for evening classes.

VII. Student Recruitment

Newspaper, radio and television publicity are used. Special motivational appeals have been developed for industry and organizations in the form of brochures and special contacts made by some departments.

* * *

Wayne State University
Detroit, Mich.
Division of Urban Extension
Total enrollment 33,000   Public Institution
Evening enrollment 12,000   Trimester System

I. Admission Policies

No deadline is set for application for admission to
evening classes. A student may register for credit courses
before transcripts are submitted. "Special" students may
take an unlimited number of hours for credit before matriculation. Admission requirements for "special" students: un-
dergraduate--none; baccalaureate degree for graduate course
offerings. For regular students, the admission requirements vary according to the various schools within the university. No ACT or CEEB scores are required for admission. Mail registration is used. Complete kits or packets
are returned to the Extension Office for pre-processing and
then they are sent to the registrar's office. The Division of
Urban Extension in "concert" with colleges formulates the admission policies for the evening students. Day and evening
students may enroll in the same class. No Orientation Program is planned for evening students. The philosophy of the
Division is "those who wish to continue to learn should have
the opportunity to do so--student achievement is the major
"screening" device.

II. Terminology

Title of Division: Division of Urban Extension. Defined: The extension of programs of the University to an
urban setting.

III. Fees

There is some difference in tuition for courses taught on
campus and extended campus courses. Graduated refund
policy is used.

IV. Faculty and Faculty Recruitment

Approximately 70-80% teaching evening classes are
full-time, but no full-time faculty members teach exclusively
in the evening. The Department Chairmen and the Director

Wayne State University (cont.)

of the Division of Urban Extension have the authority to hire full- and part-time faculty. No more than one course per term may be taught on an overload basis.

V. Scheduling

The Director of Urban Extension is responsible for the evening class schedule which is based on the "interest and goals of the students and availability of faculty." Three-hour classes meet one night per week. Day and evening classes are equal in quality. Part-time extension students are not eligible for the Dean's List.

VI. General

Students have little opportunity to discuss the academic program except by informal discussion. Adequate stress and financial support is given to the evening program. The Director of Urban Extension is responsible to the Dean and the Vice-President for Academic Affairs.

VII. Student Recruitment

Newspaper ads and news stories are used for publicity as well as radio and television. Contacts are made with business and industry and also with various civic organizations to publicize the special programs offered by the Division.

* * *

Western New England College
Springfield, Mass.
Evening Division

Total enrollment 3,000   Private Institution
Evening enrollment 2,003   Semester System

I. Admission Policies

There is no deadline for application for admission to evening classes. A student may register for credit courses before transcripts are submitted. "Special" students may take a maximum of 36 hours before matriculation. Admission requirements for "special" students include the ability to handle the course offered. Regular students must have 16 acceptable units of high school credit (each degree has particular demands). No ACT or CEEB scores are required for admission. No mail registration is used. Retention policies: Two years on probation--then separation from college. A second separation is permanent. The Director of Admissions formulates the admission policies for evening students with the advice and consent of the Academic Deans. Day and evening students may enroll in the same classes. No Orientation Program is held for evening students.

II. Terminology

Title of Division: Evening Division of WNEC.

III. Fees

Fees for day and evening students are about the same, with the exception that day students pay a "lump" sum and evening students pay $40 per sem. hr. Refund policy: A refund schedule varying from 100%-0% during the first 5 weeks of classes, but only to those with medical excuses or those required by employment changes to leave the area.

IV. Faculty and Faculty Recruitment

Every day faculty member, with few exceptions, is expected to teach one and only one evening class at extra pay. Approximately 40% of the faculty teaching evening classes are full-time, but no full-time faculty members teach exclusively in the evening. The "Dean" of the subject matter field has the final authority for hiring full and part-time faculty members for evening classes, with the advice and consent of the Evening Director.

V. Scheduling

The Director of the Evening Division is responsible for the evening class schedule. Students tentatively select courses for next year in March. The results dictate next year's schedule. Engineering classes in Mathematics, Physics and Graphics meet twice a week for one hour and a

247

Western New England College (cont.)

quarter each session. All other classes meet once a week
for two and one-half actual hours. A study by the school of
the student body involved in the twice-a-week sessions shows
an overwhelming (96%) preference for this pattern. Comparison of day and evening classes: "Evening classes are better
--students are more serious minded." Part-time evening students who register for a full year's program of 18 credits
are eligible for the Dean's List if they attain a GPA of 3.00.

VI. General

Students have very little opportunity to participate in
any discussions regarding the academic program. Innovative
practices: Calculus and Physics are studied together for half
a night each, twice a week. The six Saturday morning
classes tried in 1968-69 have proved so popular that we will
have sixteen scheduled for next year. The division now defi-
nitely operates 6 days of the week. The Director of the Evening Division is responsible to the Academic Vice-President.

VII. Student Recruitment

News stories and ads are used for publicity purposes
as well as the radio and television, and various mailings to
business and industry.

* * *

College of William and Mary
Williamsburg, Va.
School of Continuing Studies

Total enrollment 4, 200   Public Institution
Evening enrollment 1, 250   Semester System

I. Admission Policies

There is no deadline for application for admission to
evening classes. Students may enroll provisionally for credit courses before transcripts are submitted. "Special" students may take a maximum of 30 sem. hrs. for credit before matriculation. Admission requirements for non-degree
or "special" students includes "evidence of good standing in
the institution previously attended." For regular students,

the regular college admission requirements for the program in which the student is enrolled apply, including the ACT or CEEB scores. Mail registration is used. Students previously admitted and in good standing submit a "Request for Mail Registration" form from the bulletin with tuition check. The office staff types necessary registration forms from the request. There are no retention policies for the non-matriculated students-- "they are self-eliminating." The Director of the Evening College with the approval of the Admissions Committee formulates the admission policies for evening students. Day students must have special permission from their Dean to enroll in evening classes. No Orientation Program is held for evening students.

II. Terminology

Title of Division: School of Continuing Studies (Evening College is a unit of Continuing Studies). Defined: Programs primarily for mature adults who find it necessary or desirable to continue their formal education on a part-time basis.

III. Fees

Day and evening students pay the same fees. Refund policies: 1. Mail registrants who withdraw prior to regular registration receive full refund minus $5.00 processing fee; 2. withdrawal prior to deadline (2nd wk) 75% refund. No refunds after the second week.

IV. Faculty and Faculty Recruitment

Approximately 90% of the faculty teaching evening classes are full-time and no full-time faculty members teach exclusively in the evening. The Dean of Continuing Studies with the cooperation of department heads has the final authority for hiring full- and part-time faculty members. No faculty meetings are held for evening faculty. Most faculty members are allowed one class as an overload for which they receive additional compensation. Day and evening classes compare favorably in quality. Part-time evening students are not eligible for the Dean's List.

V. Scheduling

The Dean of the School of Continuing Studies is responsible for the evening class schedule. The evening class schedule is based on estimated student needs, available faculty, etc. The Dean has the authority to revise the evening class schedule. Three credit hour classes are scheduled one night a week. Part-time evening students are not eligible for the Dean's List.

College of William and Mary (cont.)

VI. General

Students have little opportunity to participate in any discussion regarding the academic program. More stress a nd financial support could be given to the evening program. The administration generally recognizes the importance and the need of the adult education program.

VII. Student Recruitment

News stories are placed in the newspapers, and given to radio and television, but the institution allows no advertising.

* * *

University of Windsor
Windsor, Ont., Canada
Division of Extension

Total enrollment 4, 200   Public Institution
Evening enrollment 1, 973   Canadian System

I. Admission Policies

The deadline for application for admission to evening classes is August 15 (fall) and June 15 (summer). Students may register for credit courses before transcripts are submitted only under exceptional circumstances. "Special" students may take 6 full courses for credit before matriculating. Non-matriculated or "special" students must be over 21 years of age and out of Grade 13 for two years or Grade 12 for three years in order to be admitted. Regular students are admitted after completing Grade 13 with 60% on at least 7 papers. Mail registration is used. The student clips the section from the brochure requesting materials for registration by mail. If the course is approved, materials are sent and the student is registered by returning them completed with a check for tuition. Retention policy: a student must pass 4 out of 6 and have a 50% average. The Senate formulates the admission policies for evening students. Day and evening students may enroll in the same classes. Additional comments on admission: "We do demand rather close counselling in the selection of each subject, insuring that it helps to fulfill degree requirements."

II. Terminology

Title of Division: Division of Extension. Defined: As an extension of the day program to those unable to attend in the daytime.

III. Fees

Day and evening students pay the same fees. Refund policy: "Diminishing by certain percentage according to weekly segments."

IV. Faculty and Faculty Recruitment

Approximately 98% of the faculty teaching evening classes are full-time and no full-time faculty members teach exclusively in the evening. The Dean of the Faculty has the final authority for hiring full- and part-time faculty members for evening classes. No faculty meetings are held for evening faculty. No overload is allowed for faculty members.

V. Scheduling

The Director of Extension is responsible for the evening class schedule. According to the Director "We try to avoid difficult combinations, and keep courses and their prerequisites on the same evening." Three-hour classes meet one night per week. Day and evening classes are equal in quality. No Dean's List is published.

VI. General

Students have no opportunity to participate in any discussions regarding the academic program. Adequate stress and financial support is given to the evening program. The Director of Extension is responsible to the Academic Vice-President. Closed-circuit TV is used for some instruction.

VII. Student Recruitment

News stories and special ads are used for publicity, but not radio or television. No contact is made with business and industry.

* * *

Xavier University
Cincinnati, Ohio
Evening College

Total enrollment 6,003   Private Institution
Evening enrollment 945   Semester System

I. Admission Policies

Students may enroll up to and including the first night
of class in any semester; for unusually strong reasons a very
few may enroll later, with the permission of the dean and
the individual teacher.   Admission requirements are high
school graduation or satisfactory scores on a battery of tests.
Some high school graduates may be rejected because of low
scores on the battery of tests; some who have not graduated
from high school, if they are 21 or over, may be admitted
if their scores on the test battery are satisfactory.   Anyone
who is on probation in another institution or who has been
dismissed from another institution must take the battery of
tests as a prerequisite for consideration for admission.   The
Evening College makes a serious attempt to collect all credentials (previous academic transcripts, application, test
scores, if required) before registration, and will not mail
grades, transcripts, etc. or send any information to a draft
board, etc., until all credentials are in the university's file.
All applicants are urged to have a half-hour conference with
a counselor before they begin their first class.   Students
with less than a 2.0 average (A=4) are first Warned, then
put on Probation, then Dismissed; the unit for making a new
judgment is, not a semester, but a block of 12 semester
hours.   Day students may enroll in evening classes, and evening students in day.

II. Terminology

Title of Division: Evening College.

III. Fees

Same tuition day and evening; but Evening College students do not pay the student activity fee.   Refunds are made
on tuition at the rate of minus 10% per week, 90% after first
week, 80% after second, etc.

252

IV. Faculty and Faculty Recruitment

About 90% of the faculty teaching evening classes are full-time and no full-time faculty members teach exlusively in the evening. Full-time faculty are hired by the Academic Vice-President on the recommendation of the appropriate dean (A&S or Business or Graduate); part-time faculty are hired by the respective deans for their divisions, including faculty hired by the Dean of the Evening College to teach undergraduate evening classes. One meeting is held at the beginning of each year for all faculty who teach evening classes; all faculty, full-time and part-time, are invited to university functions. Overload is permitted to full-time faculty only by way of very unusual exception.

V. Scheduling

The dean of the Evening College arranges his own schedule, after consultation with the other deans in order to help serve the other divisions of the university; but the evening dean has final control of his own schedule. In preparing that schedule the dean works from a master schedule which is designed so that students can look ahead and anticipate the sequence of their courses, and so that classes are evenly distributed throughout the week, and that conflicts can more easily be avoided. A Dean's List is published.

VI. General

The university does have a commitment to evening, part-time, and adult education, and to these it gives adequate financial assistance; but the primary undergraduate interest is the full-time day undergraduates. Students have no representation on councils, committees, etc., but the Evening College encourages an "open door" office, particularly for access to the dean. The dean is accountable to the Vice-President of Academic Affairs.

VII. Student Recruitment

Principally by word of mouth from satisfied students. Also newspaper ads, appearance at college nights. Special mailings to business and industry.

* * *

253